AF256173

KNOWING GOD

That I may Know Him and the power of His resurrection.

PHILIP O. AKINYEMI

KNOWING GOD
Copyright © 2016 Philip O. Akinyemi

Author's Contact Email:
feedmypeope365@gmail.com

ISBN: 978-0-9979238-2-7

Visit the author's website at:
www.fmp365.org

Printed in the United States of America

DEDICATION

To the ONE and ONLY true and living God, who in His kindness has made Himself known unto mankind—unto You be all the glory!

To my children and grandchildren.

ACKNOWLEDGEMENTS

I wish to express my deep gratitude to the following:

Pastor Emmanuel Ayorinde, the senior pastor of Christ the King Miracle Church, Redford, Michigan, whom I served under as an assistant pastor and who read the manuscript and wrote the foreword to this book.

Overseer Michael Aguda, my brother-in-law, who read the manuscript and offered comments.

Dr. Jacob Akinyemi, my younger brother, who read the manuscript and offered suggestions.

TABLE OF CONTENTS

FOREWORD

Pastor Philip Akinyemi has written a most timely reminder for the children of God, which is also good information for new enquirers, regarding the all-important subject of knowing God. He highlights to everyone the displeasure of God at human beings not knowing Him. He diligently explains what knowing God really means. We are directed to the centrality, in the heart of God, of the knowledge and understanding of Him. The learned pastor then underscores the awesome attributes of God, and outlines effective ways for us to "advertise" God.

This compact book is refreshing and avoids tedium. I highly recommend it for devotion and study. Pastor Philip is to be congratulated for this effort, which has clearly been inspired by the Spirit of God.

Emmanuel Ayorinde, PhD, P.E.
Senior Pastor
Christ the King Miracle Church
Redford, Michigan

INTRODUCTION

God loves to have fellowship with His people. This has been true since the creation; not until man tumbled into transgression was the relationship disrupted. In Genesis we read that God came to the garden in the cool of the day to be with Adam and Eve, but due to sin, they hid themselves from God. Sin opened a chasm between God and man, because God is holy.

In the course of time, God found a man called Abraham who loved and worshipped the true and living God. He was called the friend of God. While other known nations in his day worshipped idols, Abraham not only worshipped God, but directed his children and his household to keep the way of the Lord, so Israel became the people of God. Because Israel worshipped God, He established distinctions between them and other nations. God gave them wonderful victories over those who oppressed them, and lavished His love upon them with great blessings.

Under the Old Testament law, when the people sinned, they sacrificed animals unto God, because without shedding of blood there is no remission (Hebrews 9:22). Since the blood of bulls and of goats could not take away sin, but only covered it, they had to do it yearly. However, at the appointed time, in accordance with God's plan of redemption for the human race, the Son of God, Jesus Christ, came down into the world. Jesus was conceived of the Holy Spirit through the Virgin Mary. He offered His own sinless blood to pay the penalty for our sin. He took our sins away, rather than just covering them as it was under the old covenant.

When Jesus was told that His brethren were looking for Him, He told them that His brethren were those who did the will of God: that is to say, believers or Christians are the people of God.

It's always God's delight for His people to know Him intimately. He has made Himself known to us through many avenues that should cause us to want to be intimate with Him. God said in Jeremiah 9:24, "But let him that glorieth glory in this, that he understandeth and knoweth me, that I am the LORD which exercise lovingkindness, judgment, and righteousness, in the earth: for in these things I delight." What gives God the most pleasure is that we know Him, understand Him, and know His character and His ways.

God wants His people to be His friends. But how can you be a true friend without spending time with Him so as to know, understand, and obey Him? One of the marks of those who know God is that they readily obey Him. Jesus said, "You are My friends if you do whatever I command you."

After you know God and you are known of Him, you become His ambassador, and it becomes obligatory for you to make Him known to the people around you in words, conduct, and deeds.

As you read this book, my prayer is as in the epistle of Paul to the Ephesians 1:17-19:

> That the God of our Lord Jesus Christ, the Father of glory, may give to you the spirit of wisdom and revelation in the knowledge of Him, the eyes of your understanding being enlightened; that you may know what is the hope of His calling, what are the riches of the glory of His inheritance in the saints, and what is the exceeding greatness of His power toward us who believe, according to the working of His mighty power. Amen.

Chapter One

MY PEOPLE DO NOT KNOW ME

My people are fools; they do not know me. They are senseless children; they have no understanding. They are skilled in doing evil; they know not how to do good. (Jeremiah 4:22, NIV)

These are words from the heart of a loving Father who wishes His people or children to know Him intimately and have fellowship with Him, but instead they are preoccupied with their own interests. God's desire is that His people will draw closer to Him so that He can reveal His plans and secrets unto them. God has a great longing for us to know Him. He would rather have us know Him than receive the offerings we give Him (Hosea 6:6).

David told his son Solomon, "Know the God of your father, and serve Him with a loyal heart." Unfortunately, many of us reverse that, and serve a God we don't quite know well.

In the first place, God made us for His pleasure (Revelation 4:11). That is to say, He made us to have intimate fellowship with Him, but "How can two walk together except they be agreed?" as the prophet Amos asked (Amos 3:3). Our Lord Jesus said, "Now this is eternal life: that they may know You, the only true God, and Jesus Christ, whom You have sent" (John 17:3). Hence, the knowledge of God is of paramount importance!

Moses' passion and desire was to know God. He was a man who had experienced God on numerous occasions: He saw the burning bush where God spoke to him. God performed miracles upon miracles before Pharaoh through him. God used him to part the Red Sea. He went to the mountaintop with God and fasted for forty days and nights, and so on and so forth. If Moses were to write his resume, as many of us do today, it would fill volumes, but note his humble prayer in Exodus 33:13: "If I have found grace in Your sight, show me now Your way, that I may know You and that I may find grace in Your sight." Moses wanted to know God intimately, so as to follow God's plans for His people and not his own agenda. The Psalmist says, "The secret of the Lord is with those who fear Him, and He will show them His covenant." Those who fear Him are the people who love and reverence Him. They cultivate the habit of spending protracted amounts of time with Him in order to know and understand Him.

As a father, I want my children to be able to explain me to others. If they are asked, "Tell me what you know about your father," it will not make me happy if all they can say is "He is a great father; he made sure we had food on our table." That does not describe my relationship with them. As a father, part of my duty is to provide for my family. My relationship with them is built on my character, the love I have shown to them over the years, my patience when they fail to meet my expectations, my counseling, and my efforts to meet their needs and guide them in the path of truth.

When unbelievers ask some of God's people to tell them what they know about their God, all they can say is, "He is a wonderful God," or "He is a miracle-working God." We know that! What can you confidently say about His character, His unfailing love, His holiness, His uncompromising love, His grace, His mercy, and His justice? You see, the miracles God performs are an outflow of His character. God wants us to know Him intimately so that we can explain Him, and only those who spend time with Him can explain Him more effectively to others. He wants us to know Him in such a way that the devil can no longer rob us blind. By knowing Him, we are persuaded that God is greater than he who is in the world. Those who know Him are unmovable, no matter the ups and downs of life, the "haves" and "have nots." They can say, like Job, "I know my Redeemer lives."

Who Are God's People?

Let's note God's charge again: "My people are foolish, they do not know Me." His charge of ignorance is to His own people, and not to all His creation. Who are His people? In the Old Testament, the Israelites were known as the people of God. They are the descendants of Abraham, the friend of God who served the only true living God. However, when we come to the New Testament, God's people are the believers—those who have been washed in the precious blood of Jesus, whose sins have been forgiven, and who are now at peace with God through the reconciliatory work of Jesus the Messiah.

When Jesus was told that His brethren were looking for Him, He answered, "My mother and my brethren are these which hear the word of God, and do it" (Luke 8:21). That is to say, God's people are those who hear His Word and obey it. We know from Romans 10:17 that "faith comes by hearing and hearing by the word of God." When you hear the Word, confess the Lord Jesus with your mouth, and believe in your heart that God raised Him from the dead, you are saved, and that is what qualifies you to become a child of God. Paul tells us in Galatians 3:7, "Only those who are of faith are sons of Abraham." The apostle John also declares, "But as many as received Him, to them He gave the right to become children of God, to those who believe in His name" (John 1:12). Peter wrote, "Who once were not a people but are now the people of God." In a way, you can say the church are the people of God. Note that I didn't name a denomination—Methodist, Apostolic, Catholic, Presbyterian, Zion, ECWA, Redeemed, Mountain of Fire, and so on. In the church, you have bishops, reverend fathers, apostles, prophets, evangelists, pastors, teachers, elders, deacons, and the general congregation.

Now, God alleges that His own people know Him not. You see, God is not saying that you don't know about Him, but that you don't know Him intimately. In the days of Moses, the children of Israel were more interested in God's mighty miracles than in knowing Him personally and learning His ways. But, as alluded to earlier, Moses had a different spirit. His great desire was to know more and more of God, and we are told that God had conversation with him "as a man speaks to his friends." In Psalm 103:7, God made His ways known to Moses, but His acts to the children of Israel. Ways are only made known to those intimate with God. F. B. Meyer's commentary describes the difference between ways and acts: "Ways, or plans, are only made known to the inner circle of the saints; the ordinary congregation learns only His acts."

The inner circle of God is made up not of those who have titles in the church, but of those who are intimate with God. These people carry the church in their private prayers and demonstrate love for the people of God. Are you more interested in acts or miracles than in knowing His plans for your life?

Our ability to trust God lies in knowing and understanding His character. When we truly know Him, we are not moved by any circumstance that may come against us, because we are totally persuaded that He cannot fail. He is not a man, that He should lie, nor a son of man, that He should repent. And we can say confidently, like David, "Yea, though I walk through the valley of the shadow of death, I will fear no evil; For You are with me; Your rod and Your staff, they comfort me" (Psalm 23:4). Or we can sing like the sons of Korah:

> God is our refuge and strength, a very present help in trouble. Therefore we will not fear, Even though the earth be removed, And though the mountains be carried into the midst of the sea; though its waters roar and be

troubled, though the mountains shake
with its swelling. (Psalm 46:1-3)

Nothing moves us; tragedy cannot. We can boldly proclaim like Paul, "Who shall separate us from the love of Christ? Shall tribulation, or distress, or persecution, or famine, or nakedness, or peril, or sword?" (Romans 8:35).

Has God Made Himself Known?

If God has not made Himself known to us, it is unfair to charge us with ignorance. But we all know that God, who is the Judge of all the earth, will always do right.

We all know how difficult it is to truly know any human being. You can only know people to the extent that they are willing to open up to you. That is why you hear husbands and wives who have been married for many years still sometimes say to each other, "I thought I knew you," if one acts in a way that the other has never seen before or thought of.

Husbands and wives may sleep in the same bed all their lives, eat together, and raise kids together, but still not fully know each other. Why?

    1. We human beings keep secrets, and are not comfortable revealing them until we have each other's trust. God has secrets too, and they are only revealed

to those who fear Him—those who obey and reverence Him—just as you would not reveal a secret or password to a casual friend or someone who has no respect for what you love or value.

2. We do not spend quality time to study each other, paying attention to how the other acts and reacts to situations, so as to understand each other and respect each other's personalities. Two people may live together without spending enough quality time to understand one another. Similarly, many go to church for donkey's years, are active in the service, yet have no true knowledge of God, because they have not taken the time to learn the character of God. You can be a deacon, pastor, evangelist, bishop, reverend father, or archbishop and yet not have the true knowledge of God.

3. Human beings can be unpredictable: hot today but cold the next day, love today but hate tomorrow. The good thing about our God is that He is unchanging—that is His character. He is predictable in character, but you may not be able to predict the way He does things. His promises will surely come to pass, though we may not know when or how; He is faithful. We are the

ones who have problems with time. He is timeless and limitless.

Now, God is higher than anyone else and no one can be compared with Him. He is set apart by Himself. Without Him revealing Himself and drawing us with His love, we have no way of knowing Him intimately. He said, "For My thoughts are not your thoughts, neither are your ways My ways. For as the heavens are higher than the earth, so are My ways higher than your ways, and My thoughts than your thoughts" (Isaiah 55:8-9).

How has He made Himself known and drawn us to Himself? God has made Himself known through many avenues as we will see later. Let's look at some examples in the Old Testament where God made distinctions between His people and the ungodly to reveal Himself so that they could be intimate with Him. None of the gods of the Egyptians, Greeks, or Romans could be compared to the true and living God; these gods were often associated with the sun, the moon, the thunder, or lusting after women, without ever loving people. The distinctions God created between His people and the others caused the ungodly to marvel and say, "Surely there is no other god who can do this."

1. God's People in Egypt

God made a distinction between the Israelites and the Egyptians in childbirth. This is what the midwives said about the Hebrew women: "The Hebrew women are not like the Egyptian women; for they are lively and give birth before the midwives come to them" (Exodus 1:19). God gave the Hebrew women quick and safe delivery because they were His people. They served the true and living God, while the Egyptians served gods like Horus, Ra, and Hathor that could not help or do anything good for them. Of course, their gods were man-made—the projections of those who worshipped them. The Psalmist's description of these gods is well stated in Psalm 115:4-9:

> Their idols are silver and gold, the work of men's hands. They have mouths, but they speak not: eyes have they, but they see not: They have ears, but they hear not: noses have they, but they smell not: They have hands, but they handle not: feet have they, but they walk not: neither speak they through their throat. They that make them are like unto them; so is every one that trusteth in them. O Israel, trust thou in the LORD: He is their help and their shield.

After several plagues came upon the Egyptians without the people of God experiencing them, Pharaoh allowed the

Israelites to depart. Then Pharaoh decided to pursue them to bring them back into slavery. The children of Israel were at the brink of the Red Sea, and there was no way for them to escape: the sea was in front of them and there were hills on both sides. But the true and living God, the God of Abraham, Isaac, and Jacob, showed up and did wonders that none of the Egyptian gods could do. He made the sea part, and the children of Israel went through the Red Sea safely. When the Egyptian army tried it, God brought the water together and they all died in the sea.

2. God's Prophet and Baal's Prophets

God also made a distinction between Elijah and the prophets of Baal and Asherah. Elijah was a prophet of the living God, and the prophets of Baal and Asherah served the Canaanite gods. Some of the Israelites had turned away from worshipping the true and living God, so Elijah said to the people, "How long will you waver between two opinions? If the LORD is God, follow Him; but if Baal is God, follow him" (1 Kings 18:21). To prove to them that God would hear His own people, Elijah suggested a test. The people gathered at Mount Carmel and brought two bulls, one for the 450 prophets of Baal and one for Elijah; the two groups would each call on the name of their god, and the one who answered by sending fire to burn his offering would be the living and true God.

The prophets of Baal called on Baal from morning till noon to answer them, but nothing happened. Elijah began to taunt them. "Shout louder!" he said. "Surely he is a god! Perhaps he is deep in thought, or busy, or traveling. Maybe he is sleeping and must be awakened." They shouted louder and did some crazy things, even slashing themselves with swords and spears, but there was no response from Baal, because he was a dead god, a man-made god.

Now it was Elijah's turn. He prepared his altar, cut the bull into pieces, and laid it on the wood. They dug a trench around the altar and filled it up with water. Elijah now made his prayer unto the God of the whole earth as follows:

"O LORD, God of Abraham, Isaac and Israel, let it be known today that you are God in Israel and that I am your servant and have done all these things at your command. Answer me, O LORD, answer me, so these people will know that you, O LORD, are God, and that you are turning their hearts back again." Then the fire of the LORD fell and burned up the sacrifice, the wood, the stones and the soil, and also licked up the water in the trench. (1 Kings 18:37-38)

And when all the people saw this, they fell prostrate and cried, "The Lord—He is God! The Lord—He is God!"

Again, God made Himself known to the people as the ever living One who can be approached.

3. Israel's Victory over the Prideful Benhadad of Syria

In 1 Kings 20, we read how God revealed Himself by giving Israel victory over the prideful Benhadad, the king of Syria. Benhadad, with thirty-two kings helping him, attacked Israel and besieged Samaria, which was then the capital city of Israel (Northern Kingdom). He boasted that he would take the silver, gold, wives, and children of Ahab, the king of Israel, and asked him to immediately surrender them to his servants. At first, Ahab was willing to surrender to him, but Benhadad requested more things, and at these unnecessary demands, the king of Israel refused. Benhadad in his pride said, "The gods do so unto me, and more also, if the dust of Samaria shall suffice for handfuls for all the people that follow me."

So, the king of Syria set a great army against Israel, but God demonstrated to His people that He is the living and true God: He sent a prophet to Ahab, king of Israel, saying, "Thus saith the LORD, Hast thou seen all this great multitude? Behold, I will deliver it into thine hand this day; and thou shalt know that I *am* the LORD." Israel went against the Syrians and had a great victory, just as God had said.

The interesting thing in this story is that the following year, Benhadad decided to wage another war against Israel. He had convinced himself that Israel won the first time because the battle was fought in a hilly place and Israel's God only had strength in the hills. So, Benhadad waged war against Israel on the plain. God, willing to prove Himself again, sent a prophet who said, "Thus saith the LORD, Because the Syrians have said, The LORD is God of the hills, but he is not God of the valleys, therefore will I deliver all this great multitude into thine hand, and ye shall know that I am the LORD." Just as God said, the children of Israel killed 100,000 Syrian foot soldiers in one day and had total victory.

This shows that the God of Israel is the true and living God, who speaks, reveals, and is willing to make Himself known to anyone who loves and seeks Him. He makes distinctions between those who follow Him and those who follow other gods. God said His eyes run to and fro throughout the whole earth, to show Himself strong on behalf of those whose hearts are loyal to Him (2 Chronicles 16:9, NKJV).

When I initially moved in with my son in the Pittsburgh area, I was uncomfortable driving around here because it is full of hills and valleys. Whenever I feel uneasy driving, I say to myself, "My God is not just God of the plain, but He has the hills also." The God that is in Michigan is the same in Pennsylvania. Maybe, in your life, you are experiencing some ups and downs; you may think God has abandoned you and life is not worth living. Don't be discouraged; don't give up. His Word is always true. "Weeping may endure for a night, but joy cometh in the morning" (Psalm 30:5).

There are other stories in the Bible about God making Himself known to His people, such as when the wall of Jericho fell because the Israelites simply walked around the city as God commanded, or when the three Hebrew young men survived the fire because they chose to worship the true and living God. God revealed Himself so that His people and even the ungodly would recognize Him.

God's Ultimate Revelation of Himself

In the New Testament we see the ultimate revelation of God through Jesus Christ. The Prophet Isaiah prophesied about the coming of Jesus more than seven hundred years before He actually came, and he said His name shall be called Immanuel (Isaiah 7:14). The angel of the

Lord gave us the full meaning of Immanuel in Matthew 1:23 when he said, "Behold, a virgin shall be with child, and shall bring forth a son, and they shall call his name Emmanuel, which being interpreted is, God with us."

When one of the disciples asked Jesus to show them the Father, Jesus replied by saying, "Anyone who has seen me has seen the Father" (John 14:8). Jesus is God incarnate. When you see Jesus, you see God. He is God the Son. Therefore, God has made Himself known enough for us to develop a close and intimate relationship with Him.

Other Avenues of God's Revelation

God has made Himself known through many avenues, but theologians tend to categorize the avenues of His revelation to man as (1) general revelation or (2) special revelation.

General Revelation

This encompasses all that God has revealed in the world around us through creation. God uses a universal method to reach every human being. Both the sun and the moon tell of the glory of God; they reveal the knowledge of God. God makes the sun rise for both the evil and the good, and we all feel the heat of the sun; this reveals His goodness. There is no place, no nation throughout the universe, where His handiwork in the firmament is not seen. The psalmist says, "Day unto day uttereth speech, and night unto night sheweth knowledge. There is no speech nor language, where their voice is not heard" (Psalm 19:2-3).

God also reaches everyone through the human conscience and heart. In Romans 2:13-15, Paul speaks to the impartiality of God when He made the Jews realize that while they were the custodians or recipients of the Torah (God's Word—ways and principles), they would not be justified unless they obeyed it:

> For not the hearers of the law are just in the sight of God, but the doers of the law will be justified. For when Gentiles, who do not have the law, by nature do the things in the law, these, although not having the law, are a law to themselves, who show the work of the law written in their hearts, their conscience also bearing witness, and between themselves their thoughts accusing or else excusing them.

Although the Gentiles had no direct access to the Torah, God used their hearts and consciences to reveal His expectations of all mankind. Since they did what was in the law, God justified them.

God has given everyone a conscience, irrespective of nationality, status, or wealth. It does not matter which era you live in—stone age, medieval, or modern. Your academic achievements, your political achievements, and the number of houses you own give you no advantage. It is only the doer of the Word that is justified.

Special Revelation

Special revelation includes several ways that God communicated His message in the Bible. For example, when the apostles wanted to know God's choice between Joseph, surnamed Justus, and Matthias to replace Judas, they prayed and cast lots. Casting the lots was the way God communicated his mind to them. The Urim and Thummin worn by the high priest were another means used to determine the will of God (Numbers 27:21; Ezra 2:63). On some occasions God communicated His message through the appearance of an angel (Genesis 16:7-14; Exodus 3:2; Zechariah 1:12; Luke 2:10-11).

In both the Old and New Testaments, God sent His message through prophets (1 Samuel 15:10; 2 Samuel 23:2; Zechariah 1:1; Luke 3:2). We have prophets like Samuel, Elijah, Elisha, Isaiah, Jeremiah, Ezekiel, Jonah, Joel, and others in the Old Testament. When we come to the New Testament, we see John the Baptist, whom Jesus referred to in Luke 7:28, saying that of "those that are born of women there is not a greater prophet than John the Baptist." We also see Anna the prophetess (Luke 2:36) and Agabus (Acts 11:28; 21:10). All these prophets spoke the Word of God as it came unto them, and delivered it with authority because they were communicating the Word of the Most High God.

Dreams and visions are also avenues of special revelation. A dream takes place when one is asleep, while a vision takes place when one is awake. Usually dreams carry more details and thus more information and explanation to the mind, whereas a vision is a single picture. One thing about this means of revelation is that God can decide to use a believer or even an infidel: that is totally God's prerogative. Remember Nebuchadnezzar, the Babylonian king; he was a godless king, yet God revealed the secret things that were to come in latter days to him, although he could not understand it. Daniel explained the dream and showed us why God gave him that dream (Daniel 2). Nebuchadnezzar himself said, "My spirit was troubled to know the dream." You know why? Proverbs tells us that "the spirit of man is the lamp of the Lord, searching all the inner depths of his heart." Since God is Spirit, He communicates to us through our spirit. No matter how bad a person may be, God can reach him through his spirit, because the spirit of man belongs to Him.

God also sent Pharaoh two dreams in a night about an impending time of abundance and great famine. No one could interpret the dreams apart from Joseph.

> And Joseph said unto Pharaoh, The dream of Pharaoh is one: God hath shewed Pharaoh what He is about to do. The seven good kine are seven years; and the seven good ears are seven years: the dream is one. And the seven thin and ill favored kine that came up after them are seven years; and the seven empty ears blasted with the east wind shall be seven years of famine. This is the thing which I have spoken unto Pharaoh: What God is about to do He sheweth unto Pharaoh. Behold, there come seven years of great plenty throughout all the land of Egypt: And there shall arise after them seven years of famine; and all the plenty shall be forgotten in the land of Egypt; and the famine shall consume the land. (Genesis 41:25–30)

God promised in Joel 2:28 that He will pour out His Spirit on all flesh, and our sons and daughters shall prophesy, our old men shall dream dreams, and our young men shall see visions. This is happening today, and we shall see more as the return of our Lord comes near.

Three Major Avenues of God's Revelation

The three most important avenues by which God has revealed Himself to us are (1) Jesus Christ, (2) the Holy Spirit, and (3) the Bible.

Jesus Christ

The first coming of Christ was to reveal God. In John 1:14, we are told that the Word became flesh and dwelt among us, and we beheld His glory, the glory of the only begotten of the Father, full of grace and truth. While Jesus lived physically on earth, He revealed these six important things about the Father:

1. The very nature of God (John 14:9)
2. The power of God (John 3:2)
3. The wisdom of God (John 7:46)
4. The glory of God (John 1:14)
5. The life of God (1 John 1:1-3)
6. The love of God (Romans 5:8).

All these were done by Jesus through His actions and words (John 2:11; Matthew 16:17).

The Holy Spirit

As the time drew near for Jesus to go to the cross for our sins, and seeing the sorrow His disciples were in, He comforted them and gave this promise concerning the Holy Spirit: "But the Helper, the Holy Spirit, whom the Father will send in My name, He will teach you all things, and bring to your remembrance all things that I said to you" (John 14:26).

So, God has given His Holy Spirit to us believers to reveal the things concerning Himself. Paul tells us in 1 Corinthians 2:10, "But God hath revealed them unto us by his Spirit: for the Spirit searcheth all things, yea, the deep things of God." The Holy Spirit gives believers the ability to distinguish truth from error (1 John 2:27). He also helps us to know and obey the many commands in Scripture so as to be intimate with the Father (Romans 6:16; 1 Corinthians 3:16, 5:6, 6:19; James 4:4).

The Bible

The Bible is the compilation of the living Word of God. It is the most comprehensive of all the avenues of special revelation, because it documents various facets of the other avenues. Without any doubt, God gave other prophetic messages, dreams, or visions that were not documented in the Bible. The apostle John explained that everything written in the Bible concerning Jesus was to help us believe that He is the Christ, the Son of God, so that in believing Him we might have eternal life (John 20:30). Hear his statement in John 21:25: "There are also many other things that Jesus did which if they were written one by one, I suppose that even the world itself could not contain the books that would be written."

We also know from the Word of God that everything recorded in it is true (accurate) (John 17:17), progressive (Hebrews 1:1), and purposeful (2 Timothy 3:15-17).

Another Distinction Coming

Jesus used the analogy of shepherd and sheep to illustrate the relationship between Him and those who know and follow Him. These are the people who in their lifetime have a relationship with Him. Jesus said, "I am the good shepherd, and know my sheep, and am known of mine" (John 10:14).

> When the Son of man shall come in his glory, and all the holy angels with him, then shall he sit upon the throne of his glory: And before him shall be gathered all nations: and he shall separate them one from another, as a shepherd divideth his sheep from the goats: And he shall set the sheep on his right hand, but the goats on the left. Then shall the King say unto them on his right hand, Come, ye blessed of my Father, inherit the kingdom

> prepared for you from the foundation
> of the world. (Matthew 25:31-34)

When Jesus comes back again in His glory, He will distinguish between those who are His and the godless. He will separate the sheep from the goats, and those who are His will reign with Him for eternity. Do you know Him (not just about Him)? Are you known of Him? Remember, you can only turn to Him while you still have breath, for it is appointed unto men once to die, but after this the judgment (Hebrews 9:27). Come to Him today and receive Jesus Christ as your Lord and Savior.

God has made Himself known through the distinctions He puts between those who fear Him and the ungodly. The marvelous thing He has done in the lives of believers should cause us to want to know Him intimately, and that is why He charges us with ignorance for not knowing Him.

Chapter Two

KNOWING GOD

Many people take knowing about God to be the same as knowing God, but that is not true. Knowing God is a relationship, and as the relationship grows, your ability to know God deepens. You increase in your understanding of God's character, His ways, and the principles by which He operates.

The fact that you know about a person or place does not mean you truly know the person or place. I know facts about Los Angeles; I can answer questions about the Walt Disney Concert Hall at Music Center; but I have not been there, so I can't claim that I know LA. Through reading or hearing about a person, you can learn facts about the person, but you don't necessarily know that person's character until you have spent a good amount of time with him or her and seen how he or she acts and reacts, not just in good times, but when things are tough. Then and only then can you claim to have knowledge of the person's character.

Likewise, if you only have facts about God without knowing Him personally, your knowledge is limited. If you know God without having learned facts about Him, your knowledge will be shallow. But surely, an ounce of knowledge of God is worth more than a ton of knowledge about Him.

Some Christians and non-Christians alike have facts about God, but have no relationship with Him, so they cannot claim to know Him. You may be capable of answering questions on biblical doctrines accurately or even serving as a Bible teacher without really knowing God. Some are excellent at theological nuance, apologetics, and hermeneutics, but do not know God, because there is no relationship or intimacy.

By no means do I disparage theology. I have respect for theology. After all, theology in its simplest definition is thinking about God and expressing those thoughts in some way. Even the atheist has some theology: he thinks about God, but unfortunately rejects the revelation of God through creation, and what his heart and conscience tell him about God. I wanted to know theology, and that was one of the reasons I went to Michigan Theological Seminary after my doctorate in engineering. However, if theology does not deepen my relationship with God or my knowledge of Him, it is nothing but a mere academic exercise. Our knowledge about God should make us want to know Him more.

Remember, God has not charged us with not knowing about Him, but not knowing Him—His character and ways. You see, the knowledge of God is our greatest need, because all our spiritual problems come from the fact that we lack true knowledge of Him. In Hosea 4:6, God said, "My people are destroyed for lack of knowledge." The NLT rendering of this same verse is "My people are being destroyed because they don't know Me." Because we lack true knowledge of Him, many are destroyed. The destruction God is talking about here is not necessarily the devil coming after you with a hammer or gun to kill you, but the destruction of your dreams and plans. The devil will keep you depressed so that you cannot function. He will try to discourage you from getting up and keep you nursing your past failures, rather than encouraging yourself in the Lord, as David said in 1 Samuel 30:6.

Jesus tells us in John 10:10, "The thief cometh not, but for to steal, and to kill, and to destroy: I am come that they might have life, and that they might have it more abundantly." To avail yourself of this abundant life, you must know Him. "You shall know the truth, and the truth shall make you free" (John 8:32). Jesus said, "I am the way, the truth, and the life" (John 14:6). The knowledge of the truth is what sets you free. So, we see that the knowledge of God is imperative.

Those who do not know God go unprotected. The Psalmist says, "He that dwelleth in the secret place of the most High shall abide under the shadow of the Almighty" (Psalm 91:1). Many of God's people do not dwell in the secret place of God; instead, they abide in bars and in the homes of harlots, and so they are destroyed. Many wonderful dreams and visions of God's people are destroyed because they do not know their God or know that the One who lives in them is greater than he who is the world.

How Do I Know That I Truly Know God?

This is an important question that every believer ought to ask, to assure yourself that you are not fooling yourself. That is why Paul tells us, "Let him who thinks he stands take heed lest he falls" (1 Corinthians 10:12). You may think you know God but be simply bamboozling yourself. You do not want to wait till the end of your journey in life and hear Jesus say, "I know you not." Jesus illustrated the entrance into the kingdom of God with a parable (Luke 13:25-28): After the Master had shut the door, some came knocking and saying, "Lord, Lord, open for us," but the Master (who is Jesus) said, "I do not know you." They insisted, "We ate and drank in Your presence, and You taught in our streets." Jesus responded, "I do not know you. I don't know where you are from. Depart from Me, all you workers of iniquity." These people will not have a part in the kingdom of God.

We have said that knowing about God is not the same as knowing God. We have also said that being born into a Christian home does not mean you truly know God. Yes, of course, you have the privilege to know about Him, but if that knowledge about Him does not translate into a relationship with Him, it will do you no spiritual benefit. So, even if you are always in church and doing this or that for God, you may not truly know Him.

When you ask some people, "Do you know God or are you a Christian?" they answer, "Of course! I was born in a Christian family, I sang in the choir, and I belong to a prayer group." These are all good, but do you have an intimate relationship with God? Some even go to the extent of saying, "I belong to the group of some great man of God." This is simply association with great men of God. Don't get me wrong—it is okay to associate with them. It is important to have spiritual fathers, but the question is: do you have a relationship with the Father of all? You may be associated with a minister, but have no relationship with the Author of the ministry. Some people read the Bible to get sermons, but have no relationship with the Author of the Bible.

God is sovereign. He can turn our wrong motives to the glory of His Name by bringing people to His kingdom. I heard a story of some people wanting to make quick money, so they set up their musical instruments and played some Christian songs and preached from the Bible. They also set up a bowl for collecting donations, and it turned out that they made a lot of money. But, as a result of their preaching, a man was saved who turned out to be a great instrument in the hand of God. Their motive was to make money, but God turned it to the saving of a soul. Maybe this is how some churches are today; out of such congregations, God can still save those who are His. And that is why no one has the right to condemn any church. Unfortunately, some ministers use their churches as avenues to enrich themselves, but God still reaches out for His own. These ministers know about God, but have no relationship with Him.

The apostle Paul vehemently sought the knowledge of God. He said he counted "all things loss for the excellence of the knowledge of Christ Jesus my Lord, that I may know Him and the power of His resurrection" (Philippians 3:7-10). He also emphasized the importance of maintaining a constant walk with God:

Know ye not that they which run in a race run all, but one receiveth the prize? So run, that ye may obtain. And every man that striveth for the mastery is temperate in all things. Now they do it to obtain a corruptible crown; but we an incorruptible. I therefore so run, not as uncertainly; so fight I, not as one that beateth the air: But I keep under my body, and bring it into subjection: lest that by any means, when I have preached to others, I myself should be a castaway. (1 Corinthians 9:24-27)

What, then, does the activity of knowing God involve? First and foremost, we must realize that God must reveal Himself before we can know him. This is what the Holy Spirit does. In John 6:44 we read, "No one can come to Me unless the Father who sent Me draws him." J. I. Packer highlighted four things involved in the activity of knowing God:

(1) listening to God's Word and receiving it as the Holy Spirit interprets it, in application to oneself; (2) noting God's nature and character, as his Word and works reveal it; (3) accepting his invitations and doing what he commands; (4) recognizing

and rejoicing in the love that he has shown in thus approaching you and drawing you into this divine fellowship.

It is said that a woman who had been in a wheelchair for many years tearfully prayed, "Lord, I could have done so much for You, if only I could have been healthy." Now, hear the astounding reply of God to her: "Many people work for Me, but very few are willing to be My friend." God values our relationship or friendship far more than our service. Relationship leads to better understanding and deeper knowledge of Him. It is from this cordial relationship that God will show us His ways, and then we will grow in the knowledge of Him.

Recall Jesus' response to Martha when she said unto the Lord, "Tell Mary to help me." Jesus answered her, "Martha, Martha, you are worried and troubled about many things. But one thing is needed, and Mary has chosen that good part, which will not be taken away from her" (Luke 10:41, NKJV). Martha was busy serving, but Mary her sister sat at the feet of Jesus learning more about Him, which developed into deeper knowledge of God. No wonder she was one of the first to see Jesus after His resurrection! She knew and believed what Jesus said about Himself. As a result of knowing the Lord better, she poured an expensive ointment on the Lord Jesus. "Then took Mary a pound of ointment of spikenard, very costly, and anointed the feet of Jesus, and wiped his feet with her hair: and the house was filled with the odour of the ointment" (John 12:3). The more we know the Lord, the better we are able to make sacrifices for Him. The Lord told Martha that only one thing is needful in life, and Mary chose that which could not be taken away from her. Only one thing is needful to fulfill God's plans for your life: to know the Lord Jesus.

This must be our yearning, to know him deeper and deeper, as rendered by Charles Price Jones in his hymn:

> *Deeper, deeper in the love of Jesus*
> *Daily let me go;*
> *Higher, higher in the school of wisdom,*
> *More of grace to know.*
> * Oh, deeper yet, I pray,*
> * And higher every day,*
> * And wiser, blessed Lord,*
> * In Thy precious, holy Word.*
>
> *Deeper, deeper, blessed Holy Spirit,*
> *Take me deeper still,*
> *Till my life is wholly lost in Jesus,*
> *And His perfect will.*

Our Need to Know God Personally

The reasons that we need to know God personally may be many, but I will consider two here: (1) we are His ambassadors; (2) we avail ourselves of His resources.

We are ambassadors for Christ (2 Corinthians 5:20). When you become a Christian, you instantly become an ambassador for Him: you represent Him wherever you live, work, or go. To be a good representative, you need to know Him well. It doesn't come easy, and you must spend time with Him and study Him. The danger of not knowing Him well is that you will share distorted views about Him. This is what the devil does: Satan has been spreading distorted views about God since the Garden of Eden. When we know God intimately, our lives, words, and actions will mimic the One we represent. To know Him well, you have to study and meditate on His Word and listen to the Holy Spirit who resides in you.

We also avail ourselves of His resources. Often, believers are not aware of their rights and privileges as children of God; this is due to ignorance and lack of intimacy with Him. Intimacy gives you the knowledge of your rights and privileges. A child living with his parents knows his rights and privileges at home: he knows he can open the refrigerator or eat bread on the table when hungry. I believe a normal nine-year-old child will not wake his mother when he is hungry and there is food in the kitchen or dining area. However, a stranger will not normally walk in and go straight to the refrigerator without asking. Children are very good at challenging any child outside the family who just walks in and goes to their fridge. Maybe this is what we should be doing to the ungodly, since they are strangers to the family of God! Many believers act like strangers when they come to God; they have no confidence that God will hear them. But the apostle John tells us:

> And this is the confidence that we have in him, that, if we ask any thing according to his will, he hears us: And if we know that he hear us, whatsoever we ask, we know that we have the petitions that we desired of him. (1 John 5:14-15, NKJV)

Most earthly fathers desire their children to do well, and so they provide an environment for them to excel. God is no different; we learned it from Him. God wants His own people to excel in their endeavors. For us to be successful, we need to know Him so as to avail ourselves of His unlimited resources. The good thing with our God is that, unlike earthly parents, He has no limitations. God is limitless. He makes ways where man says there is no way. His resources are at our disposal.

God wants us to prosper and succeed in whatever He assigns us to do in life. The Psalmist says the Lord takes pleasure in the prosperity of His servant (Psalm 35:27). When people hear the word "prosperity," their minds go straight to money or material things. However, prosperity is more than material things. God is not against you having financial success, but the problem comes when money has you. Money is just a tool. The love of it is the root of evil, not having it, since it is just a tool. God expects us to use it for His glory and the expansion of His Kingdom on earth. God expects us to be faithful with the unrighteous mammon so that He can give us the riches (Luke 16:11). To be prosperous includes a sense of well-being or wholeness, contentment, health, love, joy, peace of mind, etc.—all things that people are earnestly looking for but cannot be purchased with money.

God opens His resources to His people, but you must appropriate them. The elder brother in the parable of the prodigal son who had been obedient to his father did not appropriate what was rightfully his, and suffered in silence because of ignorance. There are many of God's people today who must learn how to access what belongs to them. God is saying, like that father, "All that I have is yours. If you had truly known Me and understood Me, you would have known that all I have is yours."

.What Are the Marks of Those Who Know God Intimately?

The marks of those who know God intimately are many, but I will consider a few of them here:

If you know God intimately, you will fear Him.
If you know God intimately, you will obey Him.
If you know God intimately, you will follow Him.
If you know God intimately, you will be quick to repent.
If you know God intimately, you will wait on Him.
If you know God intimately, you will be free from the fear of men.
If you know God intimately, you will not quit in times of adversity.
If you know God intimately, you will make Jesus the Lord of your life.

1. They Fear God

When we hear the word "fear" we think of terror, like running from a wild animal or poisonous snake. But the Bible phrase "fear of the Lord" for His people has nothing to do with terror: it is the fear of reverence. After all, God created us for His pleasure and intimate friendship. Why would God say His secret is with them that fear Him? Why would we want to come near Him if He were a source of terror? If you love someone, you are not afraid of that person, as long as your hands are clean.

Children run to their parents when they come in, except when they have done something bad; then they hide like Adam and Eve did. Before Adam sinned, they had open fellowship with God. God came to them in the cool of the day, and I believe they must have had discussions and probably told God how much they enjoyed the fruits in the Garden.

The book of Proverbs gives us insights into the fear of God: it is "the beginning of wisdom" (Proverbs 9:10); "strong confidence" (Proverbs 14:26); "a fountain of life" (Proverbs 14:27); and "to hate evil" (Proverbs 8:13). When we fear God, we hate evil, because we do not want to offend Him; we do not want to do anything that displeases Him.

Take, for example, what Joseph said when he was tempted by Potiphar's wife in trying to lure him into committing fornication with her: "How then can I do this great wickedness, and sin against God?" Because Joseph feared God, though he was a young man, he refused to have sex with this woman. How many of God's people today would have failed that trial, and come up with excuses to justify why they did it? In Genesis 42:18, Joseph said, "For I fear God." No wonder God revealed His secret to Joseph. You do not reveal your secrets to a casual friend, but to an intimate friend. Joseph knew that God hates sin, so he refused to succumb to the advances of Potiphar's wife. He was saying, "I would rather displease you than displease my God." This is wisdom! And the Bible tells us, the fear of the Lord is the beginning of knowledge and wisdom (Proverbs 1:7; 9:10).

2. *They Readily Obey God*

Those who know their God intimately exhibit a readiness to obey His Word. Jesus in His teachings tied obedience to loving Him and His Father. In John 14:15, Jesus said, "If you love Me, keep My commandments," and in John 14:21, "He who has My commandments and keeps them, it is he who loves Me." Jesus calls those who obey His commandments His friends (John 15:10).

What are His commandments? Jesus summarized them as loving the Lord with all your heart, with all your soul, and with all your mind, and loving your neighbor as yourself (Matthew 22:37-39). That must be why the apostle John bluntly said, "He who does not love does not know God, for God is love" (1 John 4:8).

If you are not willing to obey God, you cannot be a good follower. In John 10:27, Jesus said, "My sheep hear My voice, and I know them, and they follow Me." Hearing His voice or keeping His sayings means the same thing as obeying Him. When we obey Him, we are telling God that we are not leaning on our own understanding, but on His. It might be hard, but that is what we have to do. People might make fun of us; it doesn't matter, because that is what God wants. I would rather obey His voice than that of man. No man can save me from eternal damnation: only God can.

Obedience is also directly related to the fear of God. When Abraham was asked by God to sacrifice his son Isaac, he did not try to rationalize it with God or try to remind God about what He had said concerning his son. He trusted God and readily obeyed Him. Now, hear what God said concerning Abraham: "For now I know that you fear God" (Genesis 22:12).

Jesus stressed obedience to His Word as a key to entering the kingdom of God. In Matthew 7:21, He said, "Not everyone who says to Me, 'Lord, Lord,' shall enter the kingdom of heaven, but he who does the will of My Father in heaven." To be blessed, you must go beyond just hearing to doing, and doing is obeying.

3. They Follow God

Those who know God intimately are true followers. The Bible compares knowing God to a sheep knowing its shepherd. What does a sheep do? It follows the shepherd. David said, "The Lord is my shepherd, I shall not want." When we follow God, He leads us to the still water and restores our souls. Jesus also said, "I am the good shepherd . . . and know my sheep, and am known of mine" (John 10:11, 14). One of the characteristics of those who know God is that they follow Jesus. Jesus is God manifested in the flesh, and when you see Jesus, you see His Father.

To follow Jesus is to totally surrender your will and your goals to Him. You let Him be the driver of your life. You let Him direct the affairs of your life. You simply say, "I don't know the way; You lead and I will follow. Wherever You lead me I will go, whether upon the mountain or down the valley. Wherever You lead me is the best for me. If I meet with difficulties or challenges, it doesn't matter; whatever You want is what I want to do." Jesus saw Matthew the tax collector sitting at the tax office, and said to him, "Follow Me," and immediately, he left it all and followed Jesus. Remember, Matthew was in a lucrative position, making a lot of money, but he left that behind and followed.

Are you willing to leave your own plans to follow Him? Are we, God's people, showing the world that we are good followers of Jesus? Gandhi, a man who admired Jesus Christ, was asked, "Why don't you become a Christian?" And he replied, "When I meet a Christian who is a follower of Christ, I may consider it." As Christians, we are supposed to be followers of Christ. Author Joseph Stowell said:

> Many of us live out our faith as though Christ exists to follow us. We come to believe that Christ exists to satisfy our

demands . . . This disguised form of self-serving religion sets Christ up as just one more commodity in life that will enhance and empower our dreams.

The disciples followed Jesus wherever He went. He led and directed them, except the son of perdition, Judas Iscariot, who followed his own will and perished.

Remember the refrain from William Cushing's hymn:

Follow! follow! I would follow Jesus!
Anywhere, everywhere, I would follow on!
Follow! follow! I would follow Jesus!
Everywhere He leads me I would follow on!

4. They Are Quick to Repent

Repentance is making a 180-degree turn from what we are doing wrong, turning toward God, and saying, "I'm sorry, Lord, I won't do that again." Some people think repentance is for the ungodly. No! In the Old Testament, Israel fell into the hands of their enemies because they refused to repent and turn away from their sins. When they eventually repented and turned to God, He sent a deliverer to them. Our God is kind. He is aware of our weaknesses; He sees our hearts and desires, and nothing is hidden from Him. That is why His Word says, "If we confess our sins, he is faithful and just to forgive us our sins, and to cleanse us from all unrighteousness." God cherishes our instant repentance.

Job and David were examples of men who were quick to repent and ask God for forgiveness. When Job realized his sin for the comments he made in his peril, we are told that he repented in dust and ashes (Job 42:6). David was known as a man after God's heart—I believe his ability to get down on his knees and confess his sin before God qualified him for that. In 2 Samuel 11 and 12, we read the record of David's encounter with Bathsheba, the wife of Uriah the Hittite. After committing this grievous sin, he plotted the killing of Uriah, and eventually took Bathsheba as his wife, and then the Lord sent Nathan to him. Nathan began with a very graphic story of two men from the same town: one was rich and the other one was poor. The rich one had many flocks and herds, yet took one little ewe lamb that the poor man had. Is that not what we see in our world today? When David heard that, he was greatly angry, and said, "As the Lord lives, the man that has done this thing shall surely die." Unfortunately, that rich man was him. As soon as he realized that, he repented. He said, "I have sinned against the LORD." God is just, so David was forgiven, but paid dearly for the sin, as we see in 2 Samuel 12:10-15.

In recent years, we have heard of priests molesting young children, and ministers having extramarital relationships with church members and hiding it for many years. These are not the marks of people who truly know God. That is why God said, "My people are foolish; they know Me not." But one who has the true knowledge of God is quick to repent, as we see with Job and David, and "the LORD is near to those who have a broken heart, and saves such as have a contrite spirit" (Psalm 34:18, NKJV).

5. *They Wait on Him*

Waiting is synonymous with trust. You wait on people you trust because you know their character, they are faithful, and they keep their word. People who know their God wait on Him. God, who is flawless in character, unswerving in faithfulness, awesome in holiness, and limitless in power, has said, "Wait on Me and I will strengthen your heart" (Psalm 27:14). The Prophet Isaiah puts it this way: "But they that wait upon the LORD shall renew their strength; they shall mount up with wings as eagles; they shall run, and not be weary; and they shall walk, and not faint" (Isaiah 40:31).

When we wait on the Lord, we must of course be patient. By our nature, we hardly want to wait. When you go to a restaurant, you do not want the waitress to keep you waiting, and when you go to the post office, you do not want to see a long line. Our culture has grown to expect things instantly. However, waiting on God means you trust Him, no matter how long it takes. The Psalmist said, "Because of his strength will I wait upon thee" (Psalm 59:9). You do not hasten God even when you feel He is slow. He planned our lives and ordered our steps—wait on Him!

While you are waiting, whether you are in prayer for healing, for a rebellious child to come back to God, or for a business, keep trusting and be patient and never be discouraged. This is the period when the enemy will want to speak into your heart, telling you it will not come to pass. If in business, for example: (1) Don't be idle. This is the time when you want to be doing something, even if you have to take on odd jobs until the door opens. (2) Don't set a time for God. If you have been with God for some time now, you know He is usually not in a hurry, but delay is not denial. (3) Don't try to devise your own way or method, but follow what He has put in your heart.

Sometimes people try to come up with a way to help God, but this often backfires, and you may miss His ultimate plan for you. Remember, for many of those who tried to do things in their own way after waiting for some time, the end did not turn out to be God's best. Abraham, our father in faith, tried to help God after many years of waiting for the promised child; he got Ishmael, but that wasn't the child God promised. Saul, the first king of Israel, could no longer wait for the priest and performed the sacrifice, and that was the beginning of his fall as a king. No matter how long the waiting, God's way is still the best, and waiting is a measure of your trust in Him.

One important thing to do is to keep praying and giving thanks to God in all things (1 Thessalonians 5:18). Paul and Silas prayed and thanked God while they were bound in prison, and the Lord sent an earthquake and all the prisoners' chains were broken (Acts 16:19-25).

6. *They Are Bold and Free from the Fear of Men*

The Bible narratives show us people who had no fear of men, such as David, Daniel, and his friends. For instance, David as a young man did not fear the giant called Goliath, the captain of the Philistine army. David said, "Who is this uncircumcised Philistine, that he should defy the armies of the living God?" David knew and was intimate with his God, so he never feared Goliath. Instead, when the Philistines arose to fight him, he ran toward them, and with a smooth stone and a sling he smote Goliath and killed him. The Lord God of *Sabaoth* fought for him, and he prevailed over the giant.

Daniel did not fear the king's decree (although Mede and Persian decrees were irreversible). The people conspired and purposely made a decree to catch Daniel: it said that no one should pray or make a request to any god or man except the king of Persia for the next thirty days, or else he would be thrown into the lions' den. After the king had signed the decree into law, Daniel went into his house, opened his windows, knelt down, and prayed three times a day unto the living God, as was his custom. They took Daniel and threw him into the lions' den, but the lions became his friends and did not harm him, because our unfailing God sent His angel to protect Daniel.

Daniel's friends, Shadrach, Meshach, and Abednego, did not fear the decree of the most powerful person on the surface of the earth, King Nebuchadnezzar of Babylon. This king made a golden image and ordered everyone to bow down and worship it, or else they would immediately be thrown into a blazing furnace. The three Hebrew young men refused to worship the idol, and they knew what was ahead of them: the burning fiery furnace. However, they were intimate with the living God and knew they must not have any other gods beside Him. Now hear how they replied to the king:

> O Nebuchadnezzar, we do not need to defend ourselves before you in this matter. If we are thrown into the blazing furnace, the God we serve is

able to save us from it, and he will rescue us from your hand, O king. But even if he does not, we want you to know, O king, that we will not serve your gods or worship the image of gold you have set up. (Daniel 3:16-18 NIV)

There are two people whose boldness and fearlessness I particularly admire, as relayed to me by my wife (of blessed memory): Overseer Malachi Aguda (my father-in-law) and Apostle K. P. Titus of the Apostolic Church. These men of God knew their God intimately, so that they were not snared in the fear of men. They both lived in the same area in Nigeria, and are now resting in the bosom of Christ.

Overseer Malachi Aguda heard from God in the mid-1940s that he should move away from his people to a new location that was not inhabited by anyone (that is, a forest). He moved with his wife and young children, not fearing the opposition of evil people, witches and wizards, or the mockery of men. Today, the place (Efo-Amuro) is a prominent town in Kogi state of Nigeria, and great men of God have emerged from it.

Apostle K. P. Titus was known as "Baba K. P.," that is, "Father K. P." He was an apostle in the Apostolic Church. He traveled both day and night from village to village for the cause of the gospel. At night, you could find him in the church alone praying, and there was no electricity at that time in the area. People would ask him, "Baba, are you not afraid of the evil people, the witches and wizards who typically operate in darkness?" He would simply reply, "They are the one that should fear me." He was certainly a terror to them, because he was intimate with God and had no fear of man. He knew the greater One was in him.

This kind of boldness in the Lord does not come overnight: it requires time with God and the consciousness that He is always with you. Always be aware that He who is in you is more than who is in the world (1 John 4:4). Jesus tells us to fear God rather than man, because man can only kill the body but not the soul (Matthew 10:28). Proverbs 29:25 tells us, "The fear of man brings a snare, but whoever trusts in the LORD shall be safe."

7. They Do Not Quit Serving God in the Face of Adversity

Many say they know God as long as things are going fine. Your bills are paid; you have a good job, good health. How about when trials come? Can you still say with certainty that you know God? For those who know their God and are intimate with Him, failures, disappointments, losses or gains, highs or lows do not matter. When the early apostles were commanded not to preach in the name of Jesus, they answered the council, "We ought to obey God rather than men." The apostles knew what was awaiting them—imprisonment with serious flogging—yet they were unmoved. Why? They knew their God and were intimate with Him. In fact, after they were beaten, we are told that they departed from the council, rejoicing that they were counted worthy to suffer shame for Christ.

Joseph in the Old Testament suffered adversity. As a young man, he was sold into slavery by his own brothers, and eventually thrown into prison for a sin he didn't commit. He could have whined and complained about why these things happened to him, but instead, he did whatever he was assigned joyfully, because he knew God and stood firm in the belief that He would never forsake him. He later became the second-in-command to the leader of the most powerful nation of that time. When his brothers thought he would take revenge, hear what he said unto them: "Fear not: for am I in the place of God?" (Genesis 50:19).

Who said it will be easy? Jesus Himself, the Son of God, went through trials for our sake. For the joy that was set before Him, He endured the cross (Hebrews 12:2). Jesus reminds us that in the world we shall have tribulation, but we should be of good cheer, because He has overcome the world (John 16:33). He also promises never to leave us or forsake us (Hebrews 13:5).

8. *They Make Jesus the Lord of their Lives*

When you truly know God and you are intimate with Him, you surrender to the lordship of Jesus Christ over every dimension of your life. Some of God's people want Jesus to be their Savior, but not to be the Lord of their day-to-day affairs. If Jesus is truly your Lord and you are intimate with Him, He wants to have a say about your marriage—how you treat your wife or how you treat your husband (Ephesians 5:23-33). Your Lord Jesus has an interest in the way you treat your employees, and how you behave as an employee and do your job. It doesn't matter whether you are a janitor or the president of a large corporation. Paul says in Colossians 3:23-24, "Whatever you do, do it heartily, as to the Lord and not to men, knowing that from the Lord you will receive the reward of the inheritance; for you serve the Lord Christ."

As one who is intimate with God, you will let Him have a say in your finances—how you make your money and how you spend it. The Lord is not against you having fun in life, but you will let him have a say concerning your amusements: the movies you watch, the books you read, and where you spend your vacations. Because Jesus is the Lord of your life, you will not be yoked together with unbelievers, because you ask yourself, "What fellowship has the light with darkness?" Some of God's people get into trouble because of the company they keep. But because Jesus is your Lord, evil company becomes abhorrent to you.

Now that Jesus is your Lord, you will pay attention to how you treat people in general. You will not judge people by their faces. Ethnicity or tribe will not be the yardstick for treating people well, because you are aware that your Lord is the creator of all, and made every human being in the image of Himself

Chapter Three

GOD'S DELIGHT

The Bible describes a number of things that delight or please God. These include a broken and contrite heart over our sins (Psalm 51:16-17), uprightness of heart (1 Chronicles 29:17), the praise or worship of believers (Psalm 69:30), dealing truthfully (Proverbs 12:22), the prayer of the upright (Proverbs 15:8), fear and hope in Him (Psalm 147:10), the prosperity of His people (Psalm 35:27), justice, loving mercy, and humility (Micah 6:7-8), and, of course, faith in Him (Hebrews 11:6). Delight means great pleasure, gratification, or joy. If we know the things that give God enjoyment or gratification, it will be wise of us to study them and make them a way of life.

As humans, we see how we react to things we delight in, such as sports, people, or food. Now that I live in the Pittsburgh area, I see how fans delight in the Pittsburgh Steelers, especially when they are winning, and they seem to be doing well this season (9:5) with two games left in the regular season. Fans wear their jerseys, talk about their games, and spend money freely to buy tickets, food, and popcorn at the games because they have pleasure in it.

Myself, I can remember how I delighted in my wife's egusi (melon seed) soup with pounded yam. When I saw that soup with vegetables, beef, smoked fish, honeycomb tripe, cow skin, and oxtail, the first thing that came out of my mouth was "Praise God!" And to fully enjoy it, I would forget about fork and knife, wash my hands, loose my belt, and just do justice to the food with my fingers. If my wife ever asked me for money at that time, there would be no denying her. Why? Because I had pleasure in her soup.

If we human beings react this way to the things that give us great pleasure, how do you think God will react when He looks down and see us pouring love on each other, fearing Him, and having broken and contrite hearts over our sins, and He sees justice in the land or when we prosper?

Truly Knowing and Understanding Him Delights God

In addition to what has been shown above, knowing and understanding God gives Him great pleasure.

> Thus says the LORD: Let not the wise man glory in his wisdom, Let not the mighty man glory in his might, Nor let the rich man glory in his riches; But let him who glories glory in this, That he understands and knows Me, That I am the LORD, exercising lovingkindness, judgment, and righteousness in the earth. For in these I delight, says the LORD. (Jeremiah 9:23-24)

What is God saying in these verses? God says that what delights Him is for us to truly know and understand Him as the Lord, and that He exercises (1) lovingkindness, (2) judgment, and (3) righteousness in the earth. God wants us to have insight into these three basic aspects of His overall character. God further tells us that He is not impressed by earthly knowledge, power, and riches, especially when not acquired in righteousness. God says that the wise man should not boast of his wisdom, or the strong man of his strength, or the rich man of his riches, but anyone who boasts should boast about this: that he understands and knows God.

It is interesting that many people chase after power, knowledge, and riches, which may bring them popularity or fame, but do not impress God. He is impressed by our understanding of Him: that we know His character as the One who exercises justice, righteousness, and kindness in the earth.

The Lovingkindness of God

The Hebrew word *checed,* translated as "lovingkindness" in the King James Version, is also frequently translated as "mercy" and sometimes "kindness" or "goodness." "Lovingkindness" as a word cannot be found in secular dictionaries. It occurs twenty-six times in the Bible, in Psalms, Jeremiah, and Hosea.

What is the lovingkindness of God? It is the divine love that God has lavished on His people in unmerited kindness by forgiving and showing mercy. I believe we cannot fully comprehend the preciousness of God's lovingkindness towards His people. His lovingkindness prompts His loyalty to His covenant even when we fail. He is truly faithful to His promises. He said in Psalm 89:34, "My covenant will I not break, nor alter the thing that is gone out of my lips." He lavishes His people with unmerited kindness by forgiving us our sins. "Not by works of righteousness which we have done, but according to His mercy He saved us, through the washing of regeneration and renewing of the Holy Ghost" (Titus 3:5).

God's Lovingkindness Is Better Than Life

I believe the Psalmist couldn't sufficiently describe the lovingkindness of God when he was in the wilderness. He did remember the power and glory of God in the sanctuary; David said, "Your lovingkindness is better than life" (Psalm 63:3). What could be better than life? We all cherish our lives; life is all we have under heaven and without it, we cease to exist.

In Psalm 69:16, he said, "Your lovingkindness is good." It is the goodness of God that leads us to repentance (Romans 2:4). When we foolishly get ourselves into trouble, God always make a way for us to get back. When the children of Israel sinned and were bitten by poisonous snakes, due to His lovingkindness, He made a way, and all who heeded His instruction were saved. When Adam sinned by disobeying Him, because of God's lovingkindness He made provision for Adam and Eve and clothed their nakedness. And He ultimately made provision for humanity's redemption through the gift of His only begotten Son.

God's Lovingkindness Draws Us Back to Himself

We go astray many times like sheep. Isaiah said, "All we like sheep have gone astray; we have turned everyone to his own way; and the LORD hath laid on him the iniquity of us all" (Isaiah 53:6). We go astray in our thoughts, and we are enticed by worldly things and backslide, but out of His lovingkindness He draws us back to Himself. And that is why God says He delights in us knowing and understanding that He is the One who exercises lovingkindness in the earth, so that we are not consumed in our sins.

God's Lovingkindness Causes Him to Hear Our Prayers

In Psalm 119:149 we read, "Hear my voice according unto thy lovingkindness." His lovingkindness prompts Him to hear our prayers. God said, "Call unto me, and I will answer thee, and shew thee great and mighty things, which thou knowest not" (Jeremiah 33:3). He has also given us His Holy Spirit to help us in our prayers, since we do not know how to pray as we should (Romans 8:26).

God's Lovingkindness Does Not Cease

God promised David that He would not take away His lovingkindness from him, nor allow His faithfulness to fail (Psalm 89:33). In like manner, He will never fail those who trust in Him. He said, "I will never leave thee, nor forsake thee" (Hebrews 13:5).

In Lamentations 3:22-23 we read, "It is of the LORD'S mercies that we are not consumed, because his compassions fail not. They are new every morning: great is thy faithfulness." Hosea 2:19 reads, "I will betroth you to Me forever; Yes, I will betroth you to Me In righteousness and justice, in lovingkindness and mercy."

God Requires Us to Show Forth His Lovingkindness to Others

In Micah 6:8, the Bible says, "He has shown you, O man, what is good; And what does the LORD require of you but to do justly, to love mercy, and to walk humbly with your God?" And also in Zechariah 7:9: "Thus says the LORD of hosts: execute true justice, show mercy and compassion everyone to his brother." We read in Hosea 12:6, "Observe mercy and justice, and wait on your God continually."

The Righteousness of God

Righteousness is defined as "the character or quality of being morally right or justifiable." Righteousness is closely related to holiness, yet it is a separate attribute of God. Holiness speaks to His separateness, while righteousness speaks to His justice.

To be righteous is to be just, lawful, and correct. God, within His own Being, is absolute in righteousness: that is to say, He does not violate any law, either within His own being or of His own making, because of His nature. Daniel 9:7 says, "O Lord, righteousness belongs unto

You." God is also righteous in relation to His creatures, meaning that there is no action He takes that infringes any code of morality or justice. The Psalmist declares, "The judgments of the LORD are true and righteous altogether" (Psalm 19:9). Daniel also said, "The LORD our God is righteous in all his works which he doeth" (Daniel 9:14). Jesus in His prayer for the disciples in John 17:25 referred to God as the "righteous Father." It is only God that is perfect in all His ways; no human can claim to be perfect.

Man's Dilemma

God's standard of righteousness is based on His nature. But no human has the inherent attributes of God, because of our sinful nature. We may work hard to keep His laws such as the Ten Commandments, but if we falter in one, we shall still be short of His righteousness; the Bible says all have sinned and come short of His glory.

To further compound our problem, the Lord Jesus said in His Sermon on the Mount that "except your righteousness shall exceed the righteousness of the scribes and Pharisees, ye shall in no case enter into the kingdom of heaven" (Matthew 5:20). If you know anything at all about the scribes and the Pharisees, you will realize that they were very religious. They studied the laws of God meticulously and were very strict in keeping the words of the laws to the smallest letter. They were not like the publicans (extortioners, unjust, or adulterers). They fasted twice a week and gave tithes of all that they possessed, yet our righteousness must exceed theirs. Peter also tells us, "But as he which hath called you is holy, so be ye holy in all manner of conversation; Because it is written, Be ye holy; for I am holy" (1 Peter 1:15-16). You now see the direness of our condition, for no one can attain the standard of God's righteousness.

God's Solution to Man's Problem

God knew what He was going to do about our situation. He is all-wise. Nothing takes Him by surprise. He is just and perfect in all His ways. What did God do? He made His only perfect Son to bear our sins, and that perfectly satisfied His requirement and standard for our righteousness. It is written in His Holy Word: "For He made Him who knew no sin to be sin for us, that we might become the righteousness of God in Him" (2 Corinthians 5:21). This is a wonderful exchange! Jesus went to the cross, bore our sin, and imputed His righteousness to us, and God does not see our sin, but His righteousness. Hear what Paul says in Romans 3:25: "Whom God set forth as a propitiation by His blood, through faith, to demonstrate His righteousness, because in His forbearance God had passed over the sins that were previously committed."

This is to say that we are made righteous in the eyes of God. We are now accepted as righteous and treated as righteous based on what Jesus did. He was made sin; we are made righteous. The sinless Son of God, who is perfect in all His ways—holy, righteous, and just—was treated as if He were a sinner, and we that are depraved and consumed in sin are now treated as righteous. What a wonderful exchange! This righteousness is a gift that you must receive by accepting Jesus Christ as your Savior to enter into the kingdom of God. "Christ in you, the hope of glory" (Colossians 1:27). This is the type of knowledge that God wants you to seek after and that delights Him.

The Divine Judge

By intuition, we human beings know or believe there must be a divine judge. We generally believe there can't be a Supreme Being or God who does nothing about the evils done by men under heaven, as though He condones them. You probably have heard people say, "Leave it unto God," or "God will judge!" What do they mean or what are they saying? Some have been badly hurt or unjustly accused of something that they have no knowledge of. They realize that there is no way in the world they can find justice, so they simply say, "Let God be the judge," because they believe there must be divine retribution. Imagine a man who served thirty years behind bars for a crime he didn't commit, or worse still, the evil atrocities done to the Jews during the Holocaust.

Yes, the Bible talks about a day of reckoning. "And as it is appointed unto men once to die, but after this the judgment" (Hebrews 9:27). You may say we just talked about the unfailing love of God, but remember, we also talked about the holiness and righteousness of God. The righteous God will not close His eyes to evils as though He condones them. Of course, He is longsuffering and not willing that any should perish, but that all should come to repentance. Nevertheless, there is an end to everything in this world.

The words "judgment," "judge," and "justice" occur more than 500 times in total in the Bible. Abraham first referred to God as the Judge of all earth when he was interceding for Sodom: "Shall not the Judge of all the earth do right?" (Genesis 18:25). God eventually judged Sodom and Gomorrah with brimstone and fire. They were engaged in gross evil: men sleeping with men. Ezekiel also tells us that Sodom had the sin of pride, fullness of bread, and abundance of idleness and did not strengthen the hand of the poor and needy (Ezekiel 16:49). Do we not have the same thing going on in our society today?

The Bible narrative describes other divine judgments. In the day of Noah, God judged the world for wickedness with a flood that destroyed mankind, with the exception of the family of Noah (Genesis 4-8). Korah, Dathan, and Abiram were swallowed up alive with an opening of the ground because they rebelled against Moses the man of God (Numbers 16:30). God also judged Israel several times for being unfaithful to Him, and they were oppressed by other nations.

The New Testament period is normally referred to as the era of grace because of Jesus Christ. Nevertheless, we see examples of divine judgments there. For example, Ananias and his wife Sapphira were judged for lying to the Holy Spirit about selling their property and keeping back part of the money (Acts 5:1-10). Where shall we hide today with what God has given us and we spend the tithes that belongs to Him? (Malachi 3:8-10). Herod was judged for not giving glory to God because of pride; after his powerful oratory speech, the people shouted that his was the voice of a god, and not of a man. He was smitten immediately by an angel of the Lord because he did not give the glory to God, and he was eaten by worms and died (Acts 12:21-23).

Jesus in His teachings proclaimed that a day of judgment is coming (Matthew 10-12). He also said the Father had committed to Him all judgment (John 5:22). Paul talked about the day when God will judge the secrets of men by Jesus Christ (Romans 2:16).

The Character of the Judge

1. *He is holy*. By God's nature of holiness, He is also just. Holiness will not let Him do anything but what is righteous. "All His ways are justice" (Deuteronomy 32:4). Job said, "He is excellent in power, and in judgment, and in plenty of justice" (Job 37:23). In Psalm 89:14 we read, "Justice and judgment are the habitation of thy throne: mercy and truth shall go before thy face."

2. *He is no respecter of persons*. God does not show favoritism (Acts 10:34). He judges the cause, unlike men, who tend to judge the face. King Solomon said, "Shall not he render to every man according to his works?" (Proverbs 24:12). And in 2 Chronicles 19:7 we read, "For there is no iniquity with the LORD our God, nor respect of persons, nor taking of gifts."

3. *He knows and sees every secret of men*. He sees and knows everything that is done in secret (Matthew 6:18). The darkness and the light are both alike before Him. He does not need the Federal Bureau of Investigation (FBI) or Central Intelligence Agency (CIA), because He knows the secrets of the heart. "He shall bring every work into judgment, with every secret thing, whether it be good, or whether it be evil" (Ecclesiastes 12:14).

4. *He is merciful.* Ezra 9:13 says, "And after all that has come upon us for our evil deeds and for our great guilt, since You our God have punished us less than our iniquities deserve, and have given us such deliverance as this." However, the mercy stops at the grave, because there will be no more room for repentance.

Justice Will Be Served

The task before a judge is to give everyone his due. God, being a righteous Judge by nature, will do that which is righteous and fair. Jesus will be the Judge (Matthew 16:27). God's final judgment runs as a two-way channel: the distribution of rewards and punishments. We see in Romans 2:6-11:

> God will give to each person according to what he has done. To those who by persistence in doing good seek glory, honor and immortality, he will give eternal life. But for those who are self-seeking and who reject the truth and follow evil, there will be wrath and anger. There will be trouble and distress for every human being who does evil: first for the Jew, then for the Gentile; but glory, honor and peace for everyone who does good: first for the Jew, then for the Gentile. For God does not show favoritism. (Romans 2:6-11, NIV)

Chapter Four

THE ATTRIBUTES OF GOD

The attributes of God are many; we only know what He reveals to us. Someone has said we may spend eternity learning more of His attributes. What He reveals to us now is for our benefit and helps deepen our knowledge of Him. The Bible tells us that "the secret things belong unto the LORD our God: but those things which are revealed belong unto us and to our children for ever, that we may do all the words of this law" (Deuteronomy 29:29).

God's attributes can be viewed as several branches on a large tree. The branches, of course, look alike, and at times cross each other; so are the attributes of God. Many of His attributes are similar, and you cannot talk of one without crossing to the other. We will consider God's grace, mercy, holiness, and love in this chapter.

The Grace of God

I was a teenager when I first heard "Amazing Grace" sung in a church outside my hometown. I saw people walking calmly and slowly to the altar. They were sober, and with tears rolling down their cheeks, and I wondered what was wrong. I thought "grace" meant the last pronouncement of the minister before dismissing the congregation. As a child, I heard some say, "What you don't want to miss in a church service is the grace," that is to say, you should be inside the church when the minister closes by saying, "May the grace of our Lord Jesus Christ, and the love of God, and the sweet fellowship of the Holy Spirit be with you all. Amen." But not until I experienced the new birth did I realize why tears were rolling down their faces and understand that grace is deeper than the minister's closing pronouncement.

John Newton, who composed "Amazing Grace," was a hardened trafficker of human beings. On May 10, 1748, as he was on a homeward voyage, steering his slave ship through a violent storm, he experienced what he was to refer to later as his "great deliverance." Just as it seemed that the ship would sink, Newton exclaimed, "Lord, have mercy upon us!"

That night in his cabin, he reflected on what he had said, and then began to believe that God had addressed him through the storm and that grace had begun to work for him. John Newton later became a preacher and a composer. Why was God's grace so amazing to John Newton? He expressed it in his hymn:

> *Amazing grace! How sweet the sound!*
> *That saved a wretch like me,*
> *I once was lost, but now am found,*
> *Was blind, but now I see.*
>
> *'Twas grace that taught my heart to fear,*
> *And grace my fears relieved;*
> *How precious did that grace appear,*
> *The hour I first believed!*

What Is Grace?

Grace is commonly defined as the goodness or love of God to undeserving people who have forfeited it. The word "grace" (*charis* in Greek) has many synonyms: favor, delight, gift, charm, loveliness, sweetness. Grace is the most important single concept in the Word of God. Why? Salvation is "by grace through faith." Paul says in Titus 2:11, "The grace of God that brings salvation has appeared to all men." Grace is the principle by which God operates. God demonstrates His grace through everything He does. Grace is based on who He is: He is holy, truthful, righteous, just, good, loving, and merciful. God's grace flows from all these attributes.

Grace is different from mercy. Mercy is God's attitude toward those in distress, while grace is God's attitude toward the ungodly and sinful. My professor in systematic theology used this chart to explain the difference between mercy and grace:

	Sin	Condition	Need
Mercy	Man is bearing consequence of sin	Man as pitiable	Divine help
Grace	Man seen under the guilt of sin	Man as guilty	Divine forgiveness

I read about a police officer who stopped a mother driving her car without a booster seat for her infant child. The officer would normally have written her a ticket for violating the law, but when he discovered the woman was in bad financial straits, he asked her to follow him to a store, where he purchased a booster seat with his own money for her. What this woman got was both mercy and grace. The officer not giving her a ticket was mercy: the officer had pity on her. She was guilty of driving without a booster seat for her infant child, but received what she did not deserve: a free booster seat from a police officer. That was grace. In this case, mercy preceded grace.

So is the order of our salvation as conceived by God: mercy precedes grace. For God so loved the world with a pitying love (mercy), that He gave His only begotten Son (grace), that the world through Him might be saved (Ephesians 2:4; Luke 1:78-79). Grace will always cost something; in our case, it cost God His beloved Son.

The Source of Grace

God Himself is the source of grace. Grace flows from Him. Grace was the key in the incarnation of Jesus Christ. John 1:17 states, "For the law was given through Moses; grace and truth came through Jesus Christ" and John 1:14 states, "The Word became flesh and made his dwelling among us ... full of grace and truth." Luke, in his account, tells us that Jesus "grew and became strong; he was filled with wisdom, and the grace of God was upon him" (Luke 2:40).

God's grace is obviously for everyone, but benefits more those who have accepted Jesus as the Lord of their lives. "As I live, saith the Lord GOD, I have no pleasure in the death of the wicked; but that the wicked turn from his way and live" (Ezekiel 33:11). As such, God has shown His grace even to the wicked, but unfortunately they have rejected the knowledge of God. Isaiah 26:10 says, "Though grace is shown to the wicked, they do not learn righteousness; even in a land of uprightness they go on doing evil and regard not the majesty of the Lord."

Grace Is Free but Not Cheap

Grace is a free gift from God. It has to be free, because there is no way we could pay for our sins, not even with our lives. In Yoruba (a Nigerian language), grace is called *ore-ofe*. It is a compound word meaning "free gift." *Ore* means "gift or favor," and *ofe* means "free." God gave us the greatest Gift, His Son. John 3:16 says, "For God so loved the world that He gave His only begotten Son, that whoever believes in Him should not perish but have everlasting life." Why? "For all have sinned, and come short of the glory of God; and the wages of sin is death, but the gift of God is eternal life through Jesus Christ our Lord" (Romans 3:23; 6:23). But how did this happen? How can God give such a gift to us?

> But not as the offence, so also is the free gift. For if through the offence of one many be dead, much more the grace of God, and the gift by grace, which is by one man, Jesus Christ,

hath abounded unto many. (Romans 5:15)

It costs God the life of His only Son to redeem us. It was free for us but not for God. Jesus had to die on the cross, and the Father had to turn His back on His Son. Jesus in agony on the cross said, "My God, my God, why hast thou forsaken me?" It was because of our sin!

So, grace is God giving His blessing to us when we don't deserve a blessing. The blessing grace brings is salvation. Ephesians 2:8 declares, "It is by grace you have been saved." If grace comes to those who don't deserve it, then we have absolutely no claim on it. God's grace cannot be bought, won, or worked for. If it could, it would cease to be grace. In Paul's epistles, whenever he is dealing with grace, he makes sure it is always in direct opposition to works and worthiness. For example, 2 Timothy 1:9 reads, "Not according to our works, but according to His own purpose and grace which was given to us in Christ Jesus before time began." Ephesians 2:9 reads, "Not of works, lest any man should boast." Grace is God's unmerited favor to those who don't deserve it.

Grace Brings Justification

Again, grace brings us justification. In Romans 3:24 we read, "Being justified freely by his grace through the redemption that is in

Christ Jesus." This means our justification is free: we got it without paying anything. God voluntarily and willingly gave it to mankind.

Justification is a legal term; no human being can justify someone who is guilty. You can pardon or forgive a guilty person, just like the president of the United States does sometimes, but the guilt does not go out of his record. Justifying someone means he is no longer guilty and he is acquitted. But, in our case, we are guilty and there is a penalty to be paid. Scripture says, "The soul that sinneth, it shall die" (Ezekiel 18:20), and in Romans 6:23, "the wages of sin is death."

How could God, who is just, holy, and righteous, declare us "not guilty" without encroaching on His character as the Judge of all the earth? Job asked, "How should man be just with God?" (Job 9:2). God did it through the wonderment of grace! Hear what Paul says in Ephesians 1:7: "In whom we have redemption through his blood, the forgiveness of sins, according to the riches of his grace."

God surrendered His Son to pay for the penalty with His blood. As it is written in His Holy Word, "He that spared not his own Son, but delivered him up for us all" (Romans 8:32). God imputed His righteousness to us sinners by His grace. Grace is His goodness and unfathomable love toward sinners. We should have nothing but severe punishment, but He declared us free. "If the Son therefore shall make you free, ye shall be free indeed" (John 8:36).

Are you free? If not, come to Jesus today, and He will make you free and inscribe your name in the Book of Life. The grace that was harmonious in Philip Doddridge's ear and wrote his name in life's eternal book will put yours there too, and you will reign eternally with Jesus, the King of kings!

> *Grace! 'tis a charming sound,*
> *Harmonious to ear,*
> *Heav'n with the echo shall resound,*
> *And all the earth shall hear.*
>   *Saved by grace alone!*
>   *This is all my plea;*
>   *Jesus died for all mankind,*
>   *And Jesus died for me.*
>
> *'Twas grace that wrote my name*
> *In life's eternal book;*
> *Twas grace that gave me to the Lamb,*
> *Who all my sorrows took.*

The Mercy of God

The mercy of God is His goodness that causes Him to show pity and compassion for the needy and afflicted. Our condition as a human race is miserable; we are dead in trespasses and sins, and we all need compassion from God. God in His mercy has delivered us from condemnation and judgment. Paul says, "God, who is rich in mercy, because of His great love with which He loved us, even when we were dead in trespasses, made us alive together with Christ" (Ephesians 2:4-5, NKJV).

As mentioned earlier, mercy is similar to grace, and the distinction is often confusing. By God's mercy, we don't get the punishment we deserve, while His grace allows us to get blessings despite the fact that we do not deserve them.

God's Mercy Deserves Our Praise

The Old Testament people of God showed their appreciation of God's mercy through songs and prayers. They recognized that the victories, provisions, protections, preservations, and many other good things they received were not due to their own goodness, abilities, or wisdom, but God's mercies. The Psalmist said, "I will sing of the mercies of the LORD forever; with my mouth will I make known Your faithfulness to all generations. For I have said, Mercy shall be built up forever" (Psalm 89:1-2). After the miraculous parting of the Red Sea for the children of Israel to pass safely and the drowning of the Egyptians in the same sea, Moses attributed it to the mercy of God in his song of praise. He said, "Thou in thy mercy hast led forth the people which thou hast redeemed: thou hast guided them in thy strength unto thy holy habitation" (Exodus

15:13). The Psalmist praised God for His mercy, and attributed Israel's deliverance from the Egyptians to the mercy of God that endures forever (Psalm 136:12-15).

Israel's song of ascents in Psalm 123 pleads for God's mercy as a servant looking unto his master for provision. The servant depends solely on his master and the handmaid on her mistress for sustenance; so should we wait on God for mercy. For on our own, we can do nothing but depend on the unfailing mercy of God. Jesus said it this way: "For without Me you can do nothing." God's mercy is tender (Psalm 103:4), plenteous (Psalm 86:5), great (1 Kings 3:6), abundant (1 Peter 1:3), and from everlasting to everlasting upon them that fear Him (Psalm 103:17).

The prophet Jeremiah, a man known as the weeping prophet because of his concern for his people Israel, would always appeal to the mercy of God in his prayers for Israel, because he knew they did not deserve it. Actually, the word "deserve" does not come into play when we talk of mercy or grace, because none of us is good enough to demand it or say we have a right to it. It is the goodness of God. In Lamentations 3:22-23, Jeremiah said, "It is of the LORD'S mercies that we are not consumed, because his compassions fail not. They are new every morning: great is thy faithfulness."

We must always remember to appeal for God's mercy, because we miss it many times. Remember how David appealed to God's mercy after he realized his sin in his encounter with Uriah's wife. In his prayer of repentance, he said, "Have mercy upon me, O God, according to thy lovingkindness: according unto the multitude of thy tender mercies blot out my transgressions" (Psalm 51:1). And as we can see in Psalm 147:11, God honors this approach. The Scripture says, "The LORD takes pleasure in them that fear him, in those that hope in his mercy."

Mercy is the goodness of God that flows naturally from Him. That is why God says we should come boldly unto the throne of grace, that we may obtain mercy, and find grace to help in time of need (Hebrews 4:16).

Categories of Mercy

The mercy of God endures forever (Psalm 136; 118:1-3), but is only everlasting upon them that fear Him (Psalm 103:17). Arthur W. Pink endeavored to categorize the mercy of God in three ways: (1) general mercy, (2) special mercy, and (3) sovereign mercy.

General mercy: The general mercy of God is toward all His creation. We read in Psalm 145:9, "The LORD is good to all: and his tender mercies are over all his works." In Acts 17:25, we are also told that God gives to all life, breath, and all things. God supplies all the needs of his creation. Jesus reminded us not to worry about our lives, but rather to trust in God. For example, God takes care of the birds in the air, and they do not sow or reap or store away in barns, and yet our heavenly Father feeds them (Matthew 6:26).

Special mercy: The special mercy of God is exercised toward humankind. We are made in His image, so He extends this mercy toward us all despite our sins. He formed us, so He knows our frame and remembers we are made of dust (Psalm 103:14). He gives all of us the necessities of life. Jesus' Sermon on the Mount reminded us not to only love those who are friendly, but to love our enemies and pray for those who persecute us. He added, "That you may be sons of your Father in heaven. He causes his sun to rise on the evil and the good, and sends rain on the righteous and the unrighteous" (Matthew 5:45).

Sovereign mercy: This is the mercy God has toward His covenanted people, those who fear Him—the believers. As we have seen earlier, His mercy is everlasting upon them that fear Him. God bestows His sovereign mercy on us because of what His Son did. It should be noted that the special mercy ends at the grave or at death, because Scripture says, "It is appointed unto men once to die, but after this the judgment" (Hebrews 9:27). At death there is no more repentance. In the place where the tree falls, there it shall be. That is why the Bible warns that "today, if you will hear His voice, do not harden your hearts as in the provocation" (Hebrews 3:15).

God Expects His People to Have Mercy Towards Others

As people of God, we are expected to imitate Him. We have received the greatest mercy possible from God. His unfathomable mercy saved us from eternal condemnation; we are to show mercy to others. This is so important to God that He said through the prophet Hosea that He desires mercy and not sacrifice (Hosea 6:6). In Proverbs 3:3, God says, "Let not mercy and truth forsake you; bind them around your neck, write them on the tablet of your heart."

The prophet Micah wrote, "Love mercy, and to walk humbly with your God" (Micah 6:8). Jesus gave an imperative statement concerning mercy in Luke 6:36 when He said, "Be ye therefore merciful, as your Father also is merciful." And in Matthew 5:7, Jesus said, "Blessed are the merciful: for they shall obtain mercy."

Jesus went on to illustrate the importance of mercy or compassion toward others with a parable in Matthew chapter 18. There was a king who wanted to settle accounts with his servants; one of the servants owed ten thousand talents (the equivalent of about ten million dollars). Since he had no means of paying, the master ordered that he and his wife and his children and all that he had be sold to repay the debt. But the servant fell on his knees and pleaded with the master. The master, seeing his condition, had compassion on him and totally cancelled his debt. The same man whose debt was written off saw a certain fellow servant who owed him just a hundred talents (about twenty dollars), and he grabbed him and began to choke him, demanding that he pay back what he owed. His fellow servant went on his knees and begged him to be patient with him, but he refused, and threw him in prison until he could pay the debt.

The mercy God has bestowed on us is enormous. We were dead in iniquities, and He quickened us and made us alive in Christ. Therefore, we owe it to God to be merciful to others and forgive them from our hearts.

The Holiness of God

Among the innumerable attributes of God, "holy" is the predominant one used to qualify Him. Jesus referred to Him as the "holy Father" (John 17:11). Holiness is His character. "Holy" is commonly defined as "set apart, separate, or sacred." When referring to God, it means not only set apart, but without equal and without comparison. He is in a class by Himself.

He is totally unique with no compare. He is not just holy, but He is holy, holy, holy. When a word is mentioned twice in the Bible, it is very important, as when Jesus says "verily, verily." When it is repeated more than two times, it is extremely important: it is beyond. This is the only attribute of God that is mentioned in the Scriptures three times. We never see "wise, wise, wise God," though He is all-wise. Also, the Third Person of the Godhead is called the Holy Spirit.

Many take holiness as the most important part of God's character, because not until we understand His holiness shall we truly understand and appreciate His other attributes such as mercy, love, and grace. For God, who is totally pure and righteous, to come to our level, into our sinful environment, and give us divine help and forgiveness is unfathomable. Those whom God has kindly shown a glimpse of His glorious throne have been terrified of the awesomeness of His holiness.

When God gave the prophet Isaiah the privilege to have a glimpse of heaven with God seated on the throne in the year that King Uzziah died, what did he see and hear? He saw the seraphs, the angelic beings crying one to another, "Holy, holy, holy is the LORD Almighty; the whole earth is full of his glory" (Isaiah 6:3). He was terrified and cried, "Woe to me! I am ruined! For I am a man of unclean lips, and I live among a people of unclean lips, and my eyes have seen the King, the LORD Almighty" (Isaiah 6:3-5). Isaiah saw God's glorious holiness, and it was beyond description. He saw his own righteousness as filthiness before Him. No wonder the Bible says, "But we are all as an unclean thing, and all our righteousnesses are as filthy rags" (Isaiah 64:6). God is holy and has no comparison.

The apostle John also had a vision of heaven, and he saw four living creatures that had six wings and were covered with eyes all around, even under their wings. Day and night they never stopped saying, "Holy, holy, holy is the Lord God Almighty, who was, and is, and is to come" (Revelation 4:8).

Job, whom God described as a blameless and upright man, who feared God and shunned evil, tried to defend his uprightness before his friends during his calamity. However, after the holy God had spoken to him and Job realized the unmatched holiness of God, he simply said, "I have heard of You by the hearing of the ear, but now my eye sees You. Therefore I abhor myself, And repent in dust and ashes" (Job 42:5-6, NKJV).

The Appearance of God in Any Place Automatically Makes It Holy

When the angel of the Lord appeared to Moses in flames of fire and Moses saw that the bush did not burn up, he turned aside to look at the strange sight. Then God said, "Moses, Moses, Do not draw near this place. Take your sandals off your feet, for the place where you stand is holy ground" (Exodus 3:5). The same thing happened when the angel of the Lord appeared to Joshua: "Loose thy shoe from off thy foot; for the place whereon thou standest is holy" (Joshua 5:15). Anywhere God steps automatically becomes holy. God can't stay in a filthy place. He is holy.

God's Holiness Has No Compare

God's holiness has no compare. He is matchless and without peer. He is alone by Himself. Moses in his song of praise to God said, "Who is like unto thee, O LORD, among the gods? Who is like thee, glorious in holiness, fearful in praises, doing wonders?" (Exodus 15:11).

Hannah, who was barren for many years, was mocked by Peninnah, the second wife of her husband. In her distress, she prayed unto God for a child, and God looked upon her and blessed her and removed her shame. She said these words in her prayer of thanksgiving: "There is none holy as the LORD: for there is none beside thee: neither is there any rock like our God" (1 Samuel 2:2).

God Himself said in the book of Isaiah, "Who will you compare Me to, or who is My equal?" (Isaiah 40:25). Absolutely, there is no comparison! The Psalmist, in consideration of the holiness of God, wrote:

> Among the gods there is none like unto thee, O Lord; neither are there any works like unto thy works. All nations whom thou hast made shall come and worship before thee, O Lord; and shall glorify thy name. For thou art great, and doest wondrous things: thou art God alone. (Psalm 86:8-10)

Other gods have mouths, but they do not speak, and they have eyes, but they see not. When there is fire or trouble, their worshippers carry them to safety. These gods are mere projections of those who worship them.

God Demands Holiness from His People

God watches jealously over His people and demand we be holy as He is holy. "Be holy, for I am holy." When earthly parents endeavor to live a good life and avoid unclean things with the help of the Holy Spirit, they expect their children to follow or imitate them. And when they see one of their children living totally opposite to what they believe and cherish, they are grieved. How do you think God feels? He has emotions too. God, who is absolutely holy, is grieved over any of His children living an unclean life. The Psalmist says, "For the LORD *is* righteous, He loves righteousness; His countenance beholds the upright" (Psalm 11:7).

You have been washed in the precious blood of His dear Son, and He set your feet on the right path, giving you life. Not everyone who sees the dawn of the day gets to see the sunset, but you spend the day wallowing in sin. This means you have no appreciation of what He has done in your life. The Scripture says, "Without holiness we cannot see God" (Hebrews 12:14).

God will not ask us to do something for which He has not made provision. How shall we get there? Thank God for His provision in 1 John 1:7-9:

> But if we walk in the light, as he is in the light, we have fellowship one with another, and the blood of Jesus Christ his Son cleanseth us from all sin. If we say that we have no sin, we deceive ourselves, and the truth is not in us. If we confess our sins, he is faithful and just to forgive us our sins, and to cleanse us from all unrighteousness.

My friend, what you have to do on a daily basis is confess your sins and trust in His faithfulness. He is just and will forgive you your sins. Psalm 103:3 says, "Who forgives all your iniquities." Note that He says "all." That is to say, nothing is left.

Also practice what Paul tells us in Philippians 4:8:

> Whatever things are true, whatever things are noble, whatever things are just, whatever things are pure, whatever things are lovely, whatever things are of good report, if there is any virtue and if there is anything praiseworthy—meditate on these things.

The Love of God

The apostle John the beloved, who provided about 33 percent of the references to love in the New Testament, reached a climax in his writings when he simply declared, "God is love" (1 John 4:8, 16). Love expresses the essential character of God.

How do we define or describe God's love? The Greek noun translated as "love" in these verses is *agape*. It is the unconditional love of God toward the human race. This love is not given because of any good thing we have done, or in return for recognizing or valuing Him, the Giver. This love flows towards us because His nature is love. Vine's Expository Dictionary of New Testament Words defines God's love as follows:

The deep and constant love and interest of a perfect Being towards entirely unworthy objects, producing and fostering a reverential love in them towards the Giver, and a practical love towards those who are partakers of the same, and a desire to help others to seek the Giver. (p. 79)

There are several things we could extract from the above definition, but here we will focus on (1) God's deep love toward unworthy beings, (2) God's constant love toward unworthy beings, and (3) God's love that is shed abroad in believers' hearts.

God's Love Toward Unworthy Beings

The perfect Being here is God and the unworthy beings are the human race. Man became unworthy when our first parents, Adam and Eve, disobeyed God in the Garden of Eden. They lost their relational fellowship with the Almighty God. Before they sinned, God would come in the cool of the day to fellowship with them. God had said to Adam, "For in the day that you eat of it you shall surely die" (Genesis 2:17), so Adam and Eve died spiritually that day.

God in His infinite wisdom and mercy made a way to restore man. Under the Old Covenant, men started sacrificing animals to atone for their sins, "for without shedding of blood there is no remission" (Hebrews 9:22). But it was not possible for the blood of bulls and goats to take away sins, so at the set time, the Son of God, Jesus Christ, incarnated through the Virgin Mary. He was conceived of the Holy Spirit, meaning He was sinless, and He appeared to put away sin by the sacrifice of Himself (Hebrews 9:26). Note that His blood put away sin, rather than just covering it as it was in the Old Covenant.

This deep and unfathomable love of God is seen in His gift of His only begotten Son to the world to pay the penalty of sin, which is death (John 3:16; Romans 3:23). What then is the requirement for salvation for anyone? Confess with your mouth the Lord Jesus and believe in your heart that God has raised Him from the dead; you will be saved (Romans 10:9). Can you imagine yourself surrendering your own child to bear the guilt of your community? The answer is, of course, capital NO! But God did, because of His love.

Most people give gifts with the hope of getting something in return. You give your used car to charity so that you can get a tax break. At least, when you give a gift, you want appreciation for it. But see what God did while we were ignorant and rebellious: Scripture tells us, "Scarcely for a righteous man will one die; yet perhaps for a good man someone would even dare to die. But God demonstrates His own love toward us, in that while we were still sinners, Christ died for us" (Romans 5:7-8).

This is deep love. And God is still saying to the ungodly, the atheist, the wayward, "Come to Me, I love you unconditionally." "As I live, saith the Lord GOD, I have no pleasure in the death of the wicked; but that the wicked turn from his way and live" (Ezekiel 33:11). Many young folks hear from their parents, "Get your act together and shape up, or else you will not receive help from us." So they simply become performance-oriented children. But God is saying, "Come as you are, you don't have to wait until you improve yourself."

God's Constant Love Toward Unworthy Beings

In talking to people about tragedies around the world, such as the tsunami in Asia, the September 11 attacks, Hurricane Katrina, and other disasters where thousands have died, and the acts of ISIS, Boko Haram, and other evil groups, I have seen some (believers and non-believers) who are not too sure of the constancy of God's love for humankind. The majority of the people believe God knew these things were coming. They obviously do not question the omniscience of God. The statement of our Lord Jesus Christ in Matthew 10:29 is definite: "Are not two sparrows sold for a penny? Yet not one of them will fall to the ground apart from the will of your Father."

But the questions that follow their admission of God's knowledge about these tragedies are "Why can't He stop them from happening if His love is unchanging toward humanity? Does He not care? Does this perspective shatter God's character of immutability, holiness, mercy, and constant love?" The answer is, of course, no. If you know the character of God, you know without an iota of doubt that God is never to be blamed for the tragedies that happen in our lives, families, nations, or the world as a whole.

Due to lack of knowledge, people tend to blame God for tragedies. Sometimes we ministers give just half knowledge to the people, and this can be as dangerous as ignorance.

I heard a story of a boy who became so bad in school and at home that his teacher had to recommend him for suspension from her class. He would bully the other kids in class and destroy their things. The worried mother took him to a Christian counselor. After a long session with the counselor, and without any response from the boy, the counselor said, "Let us talk to God through prayer." The boy ran out with a shout: "I don't want to talk to God!" The counselor asked why, and the boy said God killed his grandmother and his cat and made his father left the family. What happened was: At his grandmother's funeral, what stuck with the boy was that God gave and he had taken away. Within the same period, his cat died, and his father left home without returning. So the boy believed God could have stopped these things from happening.

You may be experiencing hardship, tragedy, or the passing away of a loved one. You must recognize that God's love toward you is unchanging. God is never to be blamed for tragedies.

In my own family, our middle child was brilliant and very promising. She had loved God since her childhood. She would spend more time reading her Bible than any of her siblings. She took part in church activities, and she was the one people looked for. Her ambition was to go to Yale, and she was up to it. When she moved from elementary school to high school in grade nine, she had science classes with eleventh-graders, and she made A grades. However, when she was finishing the tenth grade, something unexpected happened: depression! My wife and I had no clue as to what it was. I had heard the word "depression," but I never knew there was a higher dimension of it. We thought it would just be a question of a few months and she would be all right, but it has been many years now without complete deliverance. Can I blame it on God? Certainly, no! Do I still believe in God for total deliverance? Of course, yes! God is surely our only hope. Does it mean God does not care? God cares and He loves.

There are those who are hurting now. Innocent children are killed. Good women are battered by their husbands. Men abandon their wives and children for younger women. Remember, God's love for you does not change, because He doesn't change. The Psalmist says, "Give thanks to the Lord, for He is good! His faithful love endures forever." God delights in those who put their hope in his unfailing love.

One thing you must realize is this: God is sovereign and does not remove contingent causes. It is true, our first parents sinned, and that caused the original paradise world to be warped so that things like violent hurricanes happen. Paul explains, "The creation was subjected to futility ... For we know that the whole creation has been groaning in the pains of childbirth until now" (Romans 8:20-22). Paul's point is that the creation itself longs for its rebirth in the new heavens and new earth. Since the fall, the earth has been under the curse of death. One aspect of that curse is the violence of nature, as seen in hurricanes, earthquakes, and other disasters. And the god of this world is Satan. But his end is near!

God's constant love is also unforgettable: When Zion complained (Isaiah 49:14-15) that God has forsaken them, God asked, "Can a woman forget her nursing child, and not have compassion on the son of her womb?" He followed the question with this statement: "Even if a mother forgets her child, I will not forget you." We all know how dear a baby can be to a nursing mother; she carries the baby for nine months in her womb, going through painful nights and days, and then comes the agony of childbirth. That is why you hear mothers shout, "Don't touch my baby!" Furthermore, God said, "I have inscribed you on the palms of My hands; Your walls are continually before Me" (Isaiah 49:16). The part of your body you readily see is your hands; this is where God has chosen to engrave your name. We know God is omniscient, so He can't forget us, but He is also very practical.

God's love is also unrestrained: Paul wrote, "He that spared not his own Son, but delivered him up for us all, how shall he not with him also freely give us all things?" (Romans 8:32). Remember what God went through for us. He turned His back to His son on Calvary because of our sin. If He allowed His Son to die for us, what else in His plan for you will He deny or restrain from you?

God's love is uncompromising: God doesn't lower His standard of holiness for those He loves (Revelation 3:19; Job 5:17; Hebrews 12:5-10). Is there any good parent who does not discipline his or her child for the good of the child? Though he may not like it now, it will serve him well in life.

There was a story we were told in elementary school of a child who would bring things home from school, such as pencils or money, and tell his mother that he found them by the roadside. The mother would pat him on the back for finding things and bringing them home, but she never took time to find out the truth. Actually, the boy was stealing them. The unchecked bad behavior continued until he became a grown man. There is a saying that your sin will find you out someday, and he was eventually caught. At his sentencing, he requested to speak to his mother, and his request was granted. He moved close to her, as though he was going to whisper something in her ear, but suddenly bit her ear. When he was asked why he did that, he exclaimed, "If my mother had corrected me while I was bringing materials home as lost and found, I might not be going to jail today." God as our loving Father corrects us for our good. God is holy, and He will not lower the standard of holiness for those He loves. He disciplines us when required. "As many as I love, I rebuke and chasten: be zealous therefore, and repent" (Revelation 3:19).

God's Love Shed Abroad in Our Hearts

God's love is not only deep, constant, and unfailing, but shed abroad in our hearts. The

NIV translates "shed abroad" as "poured out," suggesting that God does not give it to us in a small quantity, but in a large quantity freely. Why does God flood our hearts with love? So that it can flow back to Him, and so that it can also flow to our neighbors.

His love caused Him to give us His only begotten Son, so there should be reciprocity: we ought to love Him back. To show Him our love, we have to love Jesus. And that is why Jesus said, "If you love Me, you will love the Father also," and "If you love Me, you will keep my commandments." Jesus summed up the commandments as loving God and loving your neighbor as yourself.

Our love for God will cause us to want to know Him better. That is why God cries through the prophet Jeremiah, "My people do not know Me." If you love your friend or someone else, you want to know them and spend time with them. In the same manner, if we love God, we want to spend time with Him through His Word to know and understand Him better. This is how God is going to reveal more of Himself to us.

Now that our hearts have been flooded by God's love, it should flow to others. God has demonstrated His love toward us; it should not be hard for us to demonstrate it to our neighbors. We should not find it hard to show love and do things for others, even if it will cost us something, because the love of God has been shed abroad in our hearts. And love must be without dissimulation—that is, without hypocrisy.

Chapter Five

MAKING GOD KNOWN

As said in Chapter 2, when you become a Christian you automatically become an ambassador for Christ, meaning you represent Him wherever you go, at your place of work, and where you live. Your words, attitude, and interactions with people should reflect God. The unbelievers should see something in you that they desire to know. What is it that gives you such peace of mind or contentment when you don't have nearly as much as they do?

How are we to make God known? Making Jesus known to the world is the same as making God known. Jesus said in John 14:7, "If ye had known Me, ye should have known My Father also: and from henceforth ye know Him, and have seen Him." Then, what do we want to tell the world about Jesus? When Jesus was born, the angel who announced His birth said, "Behold, I bring you good tidings of great joy, which shall be to all people. For unto you is born this day in the city of David a Saviour, which is Christ the Lord" (Luke 2:10-11). People must hear about the salvation God has provided through His Son, Jesus Christ.

The world that was dead in trespasses and sins now has a Savior and a Redeemer. Praise God! This is the "good news" that everyone should know, and this good news is called the Gospel. The proclamation or communication of this good news is called evangelism, derived from the Greek word *euaggelion,* which means "bring good news" or "preach." As the ambassadors of Christ, we must bring the Gospel to the dying world so that others might have eternal life. Jesus said, "And this is life eternal, that they might know thee the only true God, and Jesus Christ, whom thou hast sent" (John 17:3).

Christ Has Commissioned Us

Jesus, who is the captain of our salvation, has enlisted us in His army, and given us a command to "go ye into the world and preach the gospel to every creature." As obedient soldiers, we must heed His command. As Christ commissioned His disciples and they went about spreading the gospel, they have handed the torch to all believers today to spread the good news to every creature. The world today has a population of more than seven billion people, and we have an obligation to reach them. Jesus, of course, has not left us to do it by our own strength, because that would be impossible. After His resurrection, before His accession to heaven, having received of His Father all power in heaven and on earth, He said, "Lo, I am with you alway, even unto the end of the world" (Matthew 28:20).

The Gospel Message

In Romans 5, the apostle Paul gives us the heart of the gospel. In verse five, we are told that God displayed His love for us despite our sins, and in verse ten, that while we were enemies, Christ reconciled us to God through His sacrificial death. Christ restored us back to God. We were wayward and undeserving, but God so loved the world that He gave His only begotten Son, that whoever believes in Him should not perish but have everlasting life.

The gospel message must include warning the world about sin and its consequences (Romans 3:23; 6:23; Revelation 20:11-15). We must let the world know God's remedy for sin— the good news (Romans 3:24-26; 2 Corinthians 5:21). And then the necessity of repentance— turning away from sin, turning toward God, and believing the gospel by faith (Mark 1:15; Luke 13:3; Acts 17:30-31; Romans 10:9-13).

Our Attitude Toward the Gospel

Our attitude toward the proclamation of the gospel should be similar to that of the four lepers in 2 Kings 7. There was a severe famine in Samaria during the reign of King Ahab over Israel, because Benhadad, king of Syria, besieged it. The famine became so terrible that two mothers boiled a child for food. But God miraculously drove the Syrian army away by making them hear a noise of chariots and horses; they fled for their lives, leaving behind all their horses, food, silver, gold, and raiment. The four poor lepers (who were outcasts because of their disease) came to the Syrian camp and found no one, but tents with food, silver, and gold. They ate and carried goods away for themselves. But hear what they said afterwards: "We're not doing right. This is a day of good news and we are keeping it to ourselves. If we wait until daylight, punishment will overtake us. Let's go at once and report this to the royal palace" (2 Kings 7:9, NIV). They hastened to the king's palace, because they knew people were suffering and dying because of the severe famine, and they had found free food.

As believers, we have received the blessings of God: we have received free salvation and eternal life. Our sins have been washed by the blood of Jesus, and God has declared us righteous. It now behooves us to spread the good news to our relatives, neighbors, and co-workers. We will not be doing right if we keep silent.

The Urgency of Proclaiming the Gospel

Not only has our Lord, the Head of the church and the Captain of our salvation, commissioned us to "go ye," but people are perishing and we have what will quicken them at our disposal. We should consider the urgency of our mission, as believers whom Christ has called to be His witnesses.

The field is ripe: Jesus used the example of a farmer who has labored to plant his crop and taken care of it until the time of harvesting. Harvest is a critical period for the farmer: if he doesn't harvest in this period, the fruit will rot and fall off. We humans have a limited time to live. It is only God that is eternal, and if anyone dies without having salvation provided through Christ, he is lost forever. We believers are the messengers to carry this gospel to the people; therefore, it is urgent and imperative to reach out to unbelievers. Jesus told His disciples, "The harvest truly is plenteous, but the laborers are few; pray ye therefore the Lord of the harvest, that he will send forth laborers into his harvest" (Matthew 9:37-38).

The Gospel brings great joy to the people: When people hear the gospel and are converted, the restored relationship between man and God brings great joy here on earth and in heaven. When Philip the deacon proclaimed the gospel in the city of Samaria and the people received his message, we are told that miraculous signs followed and there was great joy in that city (Acts 8:4-8). Jesus also tells us that there is more joy in heaven over one sinner who repents than over 99 righteous persons who do not need to repent (Luke 15:7).

People are hungry and dying for spiritual food: Jesus repeatedly said in John 6, "I am the bread of life." The world is in need of this spiritual food that can satisfy spiritual hunger and thirst. But how shall the world hear this good news? Paul gives us the answer in Romans 10 with another question, "How shall they hear without a preacher?" The four lepers said, "We're not doing right, this is a day of good news and we are keeping it to ourselves." We too as believers will not be doing right if we do not tell our neighbors, friends, and relatives what God has done in our lives, so that they too will come to Christ. "How beautiful are the feet of them that preach the gospel of peace, and bring glad tidings of good things ... faith comes by hearing, and hearing by the word of God" (Romans 10:15, 17).

The Gospel is urgent because the night comes when no man can work: While Jesus was physically in this world, the work of His Father was His priority. He told the people, "I must work the works of Him who sent Me while it is day; because the night is coming when no one can work." Again, He reminds people that the kingdom of God is at hand: repent, and believe the gospel. Paul puts it this way: "Preach the word; be instant in season and out of season" (2 Timothy 4:2).

Anna L. Coghill wrote this beautiful hymn at 18 years old to reflect the words of our Lord in John 9:4:

Work, for the night is coming,
Work through the morning hours;
Work while the dew is sparkling,
Work 'mid springing flowers;
Work when the day grows brighter,
Work in the glowing sun;
Work, for the night is coming,
When man's work is done.

Work, for the night is coming'
Work through the sunny noon
Fill brightest hours with labor,
Rest comes sure and soon.
Give every flying minute,
Something to keep in store;
Work, for the night is coming,
When man works no more.

Work, for the night is coming,
Under the sunset skies;
While their bright tints are glowing,
Work, for daylight flies.
Work till the last beam fadeth,
Fadeth to shine no more;
Work, while the night is darkening,
When man's work is o'er.

Our Preparation

To grow in our Christian faith, and become effective witnesses for the Lord, it is vitally important that we cultivate certain habits in our daily lives. These include daily prayer, study, and meditation on the Word of God. We must also include fellowship with other believers, as we are told in Hebrews 10:25 not to forsake the assembling of ourselves together. The first-century believers understood the importance of fellowshipping with each other. We read in Acts 2:46, "They, continuing daily with one accord in the temple, and breaking bread from house to house, did eat their meat with gladness and singleness of heart." And what followed? They had favor with people, and the Lord added more who were saved to their number daily.

We Must Be Empowered by the Holy Spirit

In order to be effective in our witnessing, we need the power of the Holy Spirit. The Holy Spirit guides and teaches us; without His power, our witnessing will not be successful. It is also the power of the Holy Spirit that convicts sinners of their sin and brings them to Jesus to have their sins cleansed. Jesus told His disciples to tarry in Jerusalem until they were endued with power from on high. And in Acts 1:8, before He went to be with His Father in heaven, He said, "You will receive power when the Holy Spirit comes on you; and you will be my witnesses in Jerusalem, and in all Judea and Samaria, and to the ends of the earth." They tarried in Jerusalem as Jesus commanded, and they received the power of the Holy Spirit on the day of Pentecost. And what was the result? After Peter and the other disciples preached, about 3,000 souls were added to the church the same day.

If you have not received the power of the Holy Spirit, these are the steps you take: (1) repent (Acts 2:38-39), (2) ask God (Luke 11:13), (3) believe (Galatians 3:14; Acts 19:2). And if you want to know more about the Holy Spirit, read my book *The Holy Spirit.*

We must remember that our mission is spiritual, and our foe, Satan, will not sit back and let us snatch his followers away. We are going to his camp to set people free from bondage, and he will fight both tooth and nail, but our God is mightier. That is why you don't give up on anyone. It is the work of the Holy Spirit to convict people of sin. After Peter preached, we are told that "they were pricked in their hearts"—it was the Holy Spirit that did the pricking.

Paul knew it was through the power of the Holy Spirit that he was able to witness effectively. Let's read what Paul said in 1 Corinthians 2:1-5:

> And I, brethren, when I came to you, did not come with excellence of speech or of wisdom declaring to you the testimony of God. For I determined not to know anything among you except Jesus Christ and Him crucified. I was with you in weakness, in fear, and in much trembling. And my speech and my preaching were not with persuasive words of human wisdom, but in demonstration of the Spirit and of power, that your faith should not be in the wisdom of men but in the power of God.

As great as Paul was in the Lord, in knowledge and eloquence, see what he said in verse one: he did not share the gospel with superior wisdom or excellence of speech. In verse three, he confessed that he came to them in weakness, fear, and much trembling. In verse four, he said, "My speech and my preaching were not with persuasive words of human wisdom, but in the demonstration of the Spirit and power."

Paul's words here should serve as an encouragement for us to share the gospel. The enemy would like to convince us that we are not adequate or qualified to share the gospel, just to intimidate us. We may sometimes feel inadequate, but it is Christ who qualifies us, and He is our sufficiency. With the power of the Holy Spirit in us, we are encouraged and empowered to share the gospel with our neighbors and co-workers.

Focus of Our Prayer in Witnessing

Prayer is very important in the life of a believer, and the need to pray always cannot be overemphasized, especially as it concerns evangelism. Prayer keeps us in communication with God and helps us to remain dependent on Him. Jesus demonstrated the need for incessant prayer while He was physically here on earth. Jesus would be alone for long hours on the mountainside praying to His Father (Matthew 14:23; Mark 6:46; Luke 5:16). His disciples saw the demonstration of power when He came out of prayer, and said to Him, "Lord, teach us to pray."

Why is our prayer so important? One of the reasons is that we are going against the rulers of darkness of this world, as Paul tells us in

Ephesians 6:12, "For we wrestle not against flesh and blood, but against principalities, against powers, against the rulers of the darkness of this world, against spiritual wickedness in high places." We overcome by depending on God through our faithful prayer. In our prayer, we are getting God involved.

Another reason for our prayer is that we make our supplication known to Him and it brings us peace of mind, even in the midst of chaos. The peace we are talking about here does not mean absence of trouble, but through it all we have peace of God (Philippians 4:6-7).

When we evangelize, we sow the seeds of the gospel; however, it is God who causes the growth and brings about the increase (1 Corinthians 3:6-7). So as we pray, we want to ask God to open the eyes of the unbelievers to see the need for salvation. Many are perishing, and yet the gospel is foolishness to them because the god of this world has blinded their minds, so that they cannot see the light of the gospel of the glory of Christ (2 Corinthians 4:4).

Jesus said it this way: "He [Satan] has blinded their eyes and hardened their hearts, lest they should see with their eyes, lest they should understand with their hearts and turn, So that I should heal them" (John 12:40, NKJV).

We must also ask God to send more laborers to the field, because the harvest is plentiful but there are few laborers. Jesus asked

His disciples to specifically pray for this need (Matthew 9:37-38). If Jesus tells us to pray for something, it is very important. And it is also consoling that Jesus would ask us to pray, when His single prayer can accomplish more than millions of ours. Jesus sees us as partners in His ministry. The Bible tells us, "Whatsoever ye shall ask of the Father in my name, he may give it you" (John 15:16).

We must also pray for boldness to witness. No matter how much Bible knowledge you have or how long you have been in the faith, there is still some hesitance to just approach people and share the gospel with them—partly due to the reclusive society we live in today, where everybody seems to mind their own business. There is also the fear that certain people might reject or ignore you, so we need courage to speak to people.

Recently, I have been praying for an opportunity to share the Word of God with my neighbors. I always see their cars parked in the same spot on Sundays, meaning they may not be going to church. I got some Christian pamphlets (tracts) and my church bulletin, and waited for an opportunity to see them coming out. As I returned from church one Sunday, I saw one of them coming out, and I said to myself, "Here is the chance I have been praying for." Down in me a battle started, and I thought, "He is going to shun you," but I knew it was not of God. I summoned courage and approached him, and just as I had prayed, he listened and accepted the Christian literature, and that gave me the opportunity to invite him to church. When we witness, our prayer does not stop there; we have to continue to pray for God's compassion on them till they commit their lives to Jesus.

In our prayer, we must also remember to thank God for any opportunity He gives us to witness for Him. And remember Paul's exhortation concerning prayers for all men in 1 Timothy 2:1-4:

> I exhort therefore, that, first of all, supplications, prayers, intercessions, and giving of thanks, be made for all men; For kings, and for all that are in authority; that we may lead a quiet and peaceable life in all godliness and honesty. For this is good and acceptable in the sight of God our Savior; Who will have all men to be saved, and to come unto the knowledge of the truth.

In your prayer, do not doubt God. He wants to answer us according to His will. And we know the will of God concerning man's salvation; He gave up His Son for this purpose. Prayer changes things, and our prayer can change the most mulish heart and set a sinner free. Jehoshaphat prayed, and their enemies were defeated. Hezekiah also prayed, and his life was extended for another fifteen years. Prayer works!

The Holy Spirit

Do you know the Holy Spirit is your loving and faithful Comforter in time of sorrow? He is a divine Person who is available 24/7 to help you. Jesus the Son of God depended utterly upon the Holy Spirit in His earthly ministry, and we must do likewise in order to be effective and successful in our calling in life.

ISBN: 978-1-60383-524-4

The consequences of our sin can only be averted by the means God provides.

God has provided salvation ONLY through His Son Jesus Christ. Any other way leads to futility and eternal death. Choose wisely! Choose Jesus Christ.

ISBN: 978-0-9979238-0-3